THE PRISON OF

Bitterness

Setting Yourself Free

THE PRISON OF
Bitterness
Setting Yourself Free

CHARLES OFORI AKROFI

Prepared for publication by:

Authoraide Publications, LLC
1603 Capitol Ave, Suite 310 A275 Cheyenne, Wyoming 82001
Office: (307) 459-1803 | Fax: (307) 224-8450
Website: www.authoraide.com

Dedication

To my wonderful wife, Grace, and our son, Joel.

Thanks for your immense understanding, support, and encouragement.

Acknowledgments

I thank God so much for this book and all the lessons He taught me in the course of writing.

I thank the following people for their suggestions and encouragement after reading through the manuscript: John Akrofi, my nephew; Eric Addae-Sakyi, Enyonam Kpoh.

Contents

PART 2 - EFFECTS OF BITTERNESS

PART 3 - SOLUTIONS

PART 4 - CONCLUSIONS

Foreword

The writer has used many practical experiences and biblical examples to identify the causes and roots of bitterness, which he aptly describes as a "Destroyer", which one "hosts" in a "cage of his heart." He alludes to the fact that when not dealt with, that cage will open, by which time the explosiveness of this destroyer could kill the one who hosted it as well as others around him. Indeed, many do not realize that bitterness is so easy to harbour and to feed, till it becomes so explosive and cause damage to oneself and those around him. He also gives practical solutions in dealing with this "killer" as dealing with a canker. The writer, therefore, has done a good work in identifying the many avenues through which this killer is bred in an individual as well as suggested how through prayer and the extensive use of the Scriptures one could deal with bitterness and its associated causes.

Throughout the many decades I have pastored a large congregation in Ghana, with international branches, I have come across many wonderful relationships that have been destroyed due to the connected silent killers of anger, unforgiveness, pride, and bitterness. Through counselling and teaching of the Word of God, as well as through the ministrations of prayer, many have been healed. However, often times many emotional and physical scars have been left behind once these destroyers were left to breed for too long. If only many will be quick to realize the evil harvest of bitterness, they will be quick to nip it in the bud as soon as they realize it is developing in their relationships. I, therefore, believe anyone reading this book will be greatly helped, not only because the one could be harbouring bitterness, but because the writer provides insights that are also useful in advising ourselves and in counselling others to avoid this silent destroyer. May the Holy Spirit help us all to learn to walk in love and forgiveness, rather than harbour bitterness in our lives.

Rev. Steve Mensah
General Overseer,
Charismatic Evangelistic Ministry.
Accra, Ghana.

Introduction

You cannot be imprisoned without a cause, and the cause can be true or false. Bitterness is like a prison where you are kept for holding on to your anger for too long, no matter the cause. Bitterness is an imprisonment of the body, soul, and spirit, which I will explain in due course. It is also like a cancer, which eats up the host, according to American poet Maya Angelou, and eventually kills it: "Bitterness is like cancer. It eats upon the host. But anger is like fire. It burns it all clean."[1]

Cancer does not kill in a day. It takes time. And let me emphasize, it is a destroyer as well. Bitterness is also like a bit in the mouth of a horse. It is a small object, but it controls the very life of the horse that wears it. So does bitterness in the life of a bitter person. It is therefore not to be entertained by any person. Many people find themselves in the prison of bitterness, and when salvation does not come their way, the result is destruction or death, spiritual and physical. Bitterness is a spirit and may look calm in its prison cage—the cage of bitter emotion—but when let out without any restraint, it becomes a destroyer if not a killer. It's like a story I read of a Siberian tiger that escaped from a zoo some years back and mauled two young men without any provocation. The Bible says in Jeremiah 4:7: "A lion has come out of his lair; a destroyer of nations has set out" (NIV). When bitter emotion is let out of its den without any control, it becomes a killer like a real lion.

When you see a lion coming out of its den, you don't wait to see what it is looking for before you do something to protect yourself. Bitterness is like a lion that the devil has released out of its den. It is looking for someone to devour. It must not be you. The story of Absalom in the Bible, who killed his brother, Amnon, is a classic example of the caged beast let out without restraint. It was calm for a season, but when the opportunity came for it to get out, the results were disastrous. Absalom was in the prison of bitterness for two solid years, unable to free himself until the killer in him came out to finish its work. You need to free yourself if you notice that you are a bitter person or becoming a bitter person. However, you cannot free yourself if you don't know what is happening to you, how it is happening, its effects, and how to avoid it in the first place. This is what this book is all about.

If the world could be free of bitterness and bitter people, I don't think it would be the way it is today. Many people in society today are bitter for various reasons, and this is destroying many marriages, families, relationships, organizations, and society in general. If you are in the prison of bitterness, you don't have to serve your full term before being released. You can have a presidential pardon—God's pardon—if only you will ask. In my country, Ghana in West Africa, every year the president grants amnesty to certain prisoners. In effect, they do not serve their full term. They receive pardon. You also need to take advantage of God's pardon and get out of your bitter imprisonment so that you can reorganize and go on to enjoy your life.

How do you feel when you taste a bitter pill or medicine? When we were children, the only effective drug available against malaria was chloroquine, given in tablets or by injection. Because the tablets were very, very bitter, some of us preferred the injection even though we were afraid of needles. Bitterness is bitter in the sense that it never makes you happy just as the chloroquine tablets never made us smile. Bitterness is a lifestyle that is lived in a bitter atmosphere or condition infested with acrimony and hatred, sealed and polished with pretence. In this pretentious atmosphere, silence shouts louder than words.

I have come across one or two people whose lives have been completely ruined as a result of harbouring bitterness and never letting it go. There was a young man who never forgave his father for abandoning his family at a time when they needed him most. His bitterness even made him hate himself as a man, because sometimes he felt he was like his father. What you go through in life in itself does not make you bitter; rather, it is said that your response is what creates the root of bitterness, the ultimate destroyer or killer of your life. The world is never a place free of pain. Jesus never promised a trouble-free life for his followers. He did not have life easy himself. His opponents were always at their possible best. You must also know that there are disappointments in life. It is not always the way you want it.

This is why I am writing this book—to expose what effects bitterness can have on a person, and how to avoid being destroyed by this destroyer, or how to deal with it if you have this bug called bitterness in your life. Many people are being destroyed by this phenomenon and yet are "unable" or deliberately refuse to do anything about it. It has really become a bit in their lives, like the bit in the horse's mouth. If you find yourself in this state, apart from applying the recommended actions in this book, it will also be helpful if you seek help from above until you are free. Let God into the situation. Let him into your prison camp, for the Bible says, he came to set the captives free. He will set you free, for if the son shall set you free, you shall be free indeed. Don't be an "anger nurse." Be a "love minder." If you don't nurse anger you will never be bitter. To nurse is to take care of a person who is sick or injured to ensure that the person does not die or deteriorate. If you refuse to passionately take care of your anger, and to feed it with hatred and resentment, it will not survive, and bitterness will not be able to grow out of it. It will surely die.

The sun shines on and affects both the believer and unbeliever. So does bitterness. How should you as a Christian deal with bitterness to differentiate yourself as a believer from those who don't believe?

It is my prayer that by the time you finish reading this book and applying the recommended solutions, the bit of bitterness will be removed from your mouth so that God can lift you up where you belong, which is not in the prison of the destroyer and killer. I also pray that you will receive your "unemployment benefits" since you will no longer be an "anger nurse." As a Christian, you have an advantage: Christ in you! Don't kill your happiness! You have to *destroy the destroyer* before it *destroys* you. Remove the bit, break the chains, and set yourself free from the PRISON OF BITTERNESS.

Stay blessed! *Invictus!*
Rev. Charles Akrofi

Chapter 1

DEFINITIONS

The word *bitter* is defined as a strong, sharp, or pungent taste that is not pleasant. It can also be something that is emotionally painful or difficult to deal with. Bitterness is retaining the effect of hurts and being resentful toward those who perpetrated whatever hurt you. Bitterness therefore expresses something unpleasant that is difficult to accept and may be met with intense hostility. It is basically the result of unforgiveness. Bitterness is anger that has been allowed to fester or ferment; it is anger that has been watered and nurtured to grow for some time—or, I dare say, for a long time. It is anger that is welcomed to stay beyond what could be called the acceptable time limit, thereby going sour and harbouring hatred, jealousy, and resentment. It is a bad emotional habit that is acquired with the continuous practice of unforgiveness over a long period. There is a Ghanaian adage that says, "When water stays in a pot for a long time, it stinks." So does anger. Bitterness is also resentment infused and saturated with grudges, which results in what

Hebrews 12:15 calls the root of bitterness dangerously heading toward enmity with God.

The Bible talks of the root of bitterness in Hebrews 12:15, which I want us to explore a bit:

> See to it that no one misses the grace of God and that no bitter root grows up to cause trouble and defile many.

> Look after each other so that not one of you will fail to find God's best blessings. Watch out that no bitterness takes root among you, for as it springs up it causes deep trouble, hurting many in their spiritual lives. (TLB)

Bitterness has the capacity to take deep root in a person's life. And when it does, it causes deep trouble and can hurt people in their spiritual lives, as the Living Bible (TLB) states. A root is the part of a plant that grows in the ground and draws up water and nutrients to feed the plant. It also holds the plant in place, and in some cases, the roots store food for future use. When bitterness takes root, it grows into the soul and feeds the body and spirit with venom from its storehouse in order to keep it in place without shaking or giving up.

When something takes root in a life or a place, it tends to become dominant and take control of that life, situation, or environment. This is the reason I talk about bitterness as a bit in the life of a person who is overcome by anger.

A bit is a metal bar in a horse's mouth. It is attached to the reins. The rider moves the bit with the reins in order to control the horse's actions. The primary issue here is control:

1.   To influence or direct through authority or dominance
2.   To force conformity

3.   To restrain
4.   To prevent dissemination

Looking at these four definitions of control (and the subsequent discussions I have put forth under the "Causes of Bitterness"), it is clear that, when bitterness takes control of a person, it exercises a dominating influence. It regulates the person's life and thinking by regulating his or her ability to relate freely; it thereby prevents the person from being free, hence imprisonment.

In Ephesians 4:26–27, we read, "In your anger do not sin: Do not let the sun go down while you are still angry, and do not give the devil a foothold." (NIV). This means that the day should not end with you still angry over an issue with somebody. As soon as another day breaks on your unresolved anger, the devil begins to smile; this is because an opening has been created for him to plant his feet firmly in the situation and take control. He takes full control of the reins that hold the bit. When the devil takes control, I know, and can assure you, that he will execute his agenda to its logical conclusion, which will definitely not be in your interest. Bitterness is one of the devil's ways of executing, as we know from John 10:10: "The thief comes only to steal and kill and destroy." (NIV). This will be explained when I talk about the effects of bitterness later. It is a destroyer!

According to Martin Luther King, "Never succumb to the temptation of bitterness,"[2] and this is buttressed by Maya Angelou when she says that "Bitterness is like cancer. It eats upon the host. But anger is like fire. It burns it all clean." Succumbing to bitterness is like being unfortunately overcome by cancer.

I would be very much surprised if I hear that somebody is happy harbouring cancer in his or her body and is doing nothing about it. Since it would be unnatural to do that, I believe bitterness should be treated with the same hatred and dislike that cancer is given. It must also be feared because it is a controller and a destroyer.

The root of a plant does not take a day to reach whatever depth it should go. It takes a reasonable time to do that. In the same way, bitterness, like a cancer, also takes time to eat up its host. So why do people get bitter at all in spite of all the dangers associated with it?

Part 1

CAUSES OF BITTERNESS

*Just as there is no smoke without a fire, so is
there no bitterness without anger.*

Chapter 2

HURTS AND OFFENSES

According to Italian writer Cesare Pavese, "If you wish to travel far and fast, travel light. Take off all your envies, jealousies, unforgiveness, selfishness and fears."[3] This is a wonderful and true saying. Unforgiveness is a dead weight around your neck if you walk in it. It is something that will impede your progress. When I look at most of the causes of bitterness, I realize that the critical issue behind all of them is unforgiveness. And in this book we will discuss some of these causes and the role of unforgiveness in all of them. According to George Bernard Shaw, an Anglo-Irish playwright, every cruel action hurts or offends somebody. He says, "Cruelty would be delicious if only one could find the sort of cruelty that didn't hurt."[4] Sometimes even a kind gesture may offend someone, so in this world, hurts and offenses will always be with us.

As I have already mentioned, one of the main causes of bitterness is unforgiveness. The natural propensity or inclination for a human being who is hurt or offended is to retaliate. But where retaliation does not take place (even though it is wanted) or the opportunity to do so does not exist immediately and there is no forgiveness, bitterness sets in with time. I am sure that many people can testify to the fact that, at one point in time in their lives, they have been unforgiving or bitter about something. The issue of unforgiveness cuts across all cultures, races, ages, religions, and social groupings. It is a human characteristic. Forgiveness does not come naturally to a lot of people. Many have to work at it no matter who they are and make a conscious effort to forgive. There is a spirit behind unforgiveness, which is not of God. And so far as you allow that spirit to control your emotions, it will be difficult for you to forgive. It is the spirit of the destroyer, the one who comes to steal, kill, and destroy—the devil.

An offense could be a wrong done to somebody, an injury caused, a stumbling block, or anything that causes temptation. An offense, of course, is something that causes another to be hurt, upset, or angry. I believe that such offenses are the commonest reason that so many people become bitter in life. It is sometimes amazing to find out that those who hurt us most are very good people we know and love. They are sometimes family members who are not too distant in relation. We are hurt or offended by these people by what they say or do—or by what they do not say or do; that is, by commission or omission, deliberately or inadvertently. And sometimes it is incredible how we can be offended by what was not said but expected. Unfulfilled expectations from life, marriage, career, friends, and other areas of life can be very hurtful. Someone told a story about a schoolboy who attacked another student right in the presence of a teacher on the street after school. The teacher could not understand why the boy attacked his friend. He did not hear the boy who was attacked say anything or see him do anything that warranted such an attack. When he demanded an explanation, to his surprise the attacker said the other boy was insulting him in his head. One may ask, how did he know? Apparently, the attacking boy had been trying to fight this youngster in class that day, but the youngster never responded and so the attacker was offended and frustrated.

Have you ever done something for somebody and expected a thank you—but there was absolute silence? What about a false accusation? Were you abused as a child, or are you still being abused, betrayed, or rejected? Have you ever been a victim of rape? Have you been dismissed from your job unjustifiably or undermined at the workplace? The list can be endless. How does it feel when it is a wife or a husband who offends, or a lover? It is unbelievable, is it not? It hurts even more.

Speaking of betrayal and rejection, let me tell you a story that occurred on a small island country somewhere in the South Pacific. Clement courted Sally, a young lady, for about two years. In the third year they decided to marry, and therefore they bought all the necessary things for their engagement and wedding. They rented an apartment and kept all their things for the marriage ceremonies there, even though they were not living in the place. Not long after, the young lady told the fiancé that she was going to travel to her village for a while. She came back after a week or two and told the fiancé that she had got an opportunity to travel abroad for a holiday and that the fiancé should continue the preparations in her absence. A few days later, Sally left the country. She called the fiancé two weeks into her "holidays" and told him that she was very sorry they could not get married because she had been wedded to someone a few weeks back in her village. She was now with her husband in another country. I can imagine you shaking your head in disbelief. Two years down the line, this young man found another beautiful girl, Christie, a Christian. After one and half years of being together, Clement decided to propose to this young woman and get married before anything happened again. A week before his scheduled proposal date, he had the shock of his life a second time. His girlfriend called one hot, humid tropical afternoon and told him that their relationship was over. How? Why? Another "devil" had crossed him. Let me ask you, does this young man have the right to be angry and bitter?

Sometimes people become bitter when they are unable to confront those who hurt them, or when the perpetrators refuse to accept the fact that they are wrong, or even do not see the need to apologize. In Ghana, there are reported cases of young girls who are raped by adults but are threatened with death should they expose the perpetrators. Will these persons not feel hurt or offended and likely be bitter all their life if there is no healing intervention or redress in the course of time? There is this saying in Twi, the language of the Ashanti people of Ghana in West Africa, which says, *"Sɛ aboa bi bɛka wo a, na ofi wo ntama mu."* To wit, "If you will be bitten by an insect, it will definitely come from your cloth." Those who offend or hurt us are usually people who are close, like co-workers, church members, schoolmates, teachers, brothers and sisters, parents, uncles and aunties, as well as those we consider friends and casual acquaintances. So far as these people continue to be around, the likelihood of us being hurt or offended will always be there.

I heard, on a foreign radio station, the experience of an unemployed, frustrated young female college graduate. In her quest to find a job, she had the unfortunate experience of having to deal with some sex maniacs who were working, respectively, as human resource manager and managing director of a particular company. The HR manager promised to give her a job on the condition that she sleep with him. When he satisfied himself, he told the lady that, if she really wanted the job then, she would have to satisfy the final approver of her employment, the managing director, too. The lady gave in to the managing director, but she received a letter a few days later saying they were regretful in having to inform her that she did not have the job. How wicked is that? Would this lady be justified if she became bitter?

On this same radio station, I heard of a man who lost his job and, in the course of searching for one, found the opportunity for temporary employment for his wife, who was also unemployed. The opening was in a company owned by a "friend" of the man. When the woman went to see this so-called friend of her husband, the condition for the job was sex with that man. The woman reported the matter to the husband expecting him to confront his friend, but the man, in desperation, surprisingly agreed. The family was in serious debt, and life was generally unbearable. After the woman got the job, this sex business did not end. The husband began to shun his wife, and she was living with guilt. She could no longer relate to her husband romantically. How do you think this woman should feel towards these two men? Your guess is as good as mine.

Here is the story of someone who was hurt and offended as a result of what a close relation did to his sister as recorded in the Bible. I will be making references to this personality quite often in this book.

When her brother Absalom saw her, he asked, "Has Amnon molested you? Please, sister, don't let it upset you so much. He is your half-brother, so don't tell anyone about it." So Tamar lived in Absalom's house, sad and lonely. When King David heard what had happened, he was furious. And Absalom hated Amnon so much for having raped his sister Tamar that he would no longer even speak to him.

Absalom's Revenge

Two years later Absalom was having his sheep sheared at Baal Hazor, near the town of Ephraim, and he invited all the king's sons to be there. He went to King David and said, "Your Majesty, I am having my sheep sheared. Will you and your officials come and take part in the festivities?"

"No, my son," the king answered. "It would be too much trouble for you if we all went." Absalom insisted, but the king would not give in, and he asked Absalom to leave.

But Absalom said, "Well then, will you at least let my brother Amnon come?"

"Why should he?" the king asked. But Absalom kept on insisting until David finally let Amnon and all his other sons go with Absalom.

Absalom prepared a banquet fit for a king and instructed his servants: "Notice when Amnon has had too much to drink, and then when I give the order, kill him. Don't be afraid. I will take the responsibility myself. Be brave and don't hesitate!" So the servants followed Absalom's instructions and killed Amnon. All the rest of David's sons mounted their mules and fled. (2 Samuel 13:20–29 GNT)

This is a classic example of how someone who is hurt or offended and does nothing to heal the hurt could end up. Absalom's sister, Tamar, was deceived and raped by his half-brother, Amnon. The Bible says that when Absalom heard about what had happened, he never spoke to Amnon, good or bad, but hated him with all his strength and all his might. He was hurt and offended. At that time, no one could tell, but subsequent events proved this assertion. Sometimes when people are hurt it is not easy to tell. They pretend that everything is all right. It is even possible that, as you read this book, you may be experiencing hurt over having been offended by somebody; however, you think you have been able to get over it. But just wait for that same person or situation to show up again—then you will really know whether you have dealt with it or it is just incubating. For two years Absalom never forgave Amnon. Unforgiveness was the key factor in every decision he took. He nursed this hatred with "tender loving care," watered it with all the venom he could muster (his thoughts and plans for the two years) till it became a big bitter bomb, which exploded like a dynamite one day claiming a victim—Amnon—and affecting many others. It was also like a bit which controlled his whole thinking. This is what I call "the Absalom bug"—the Absalom disease. He never forgave his half-brother all this while.

The Bible says, in Matthew 18:7, "Woe to the world because of the things that cause people to stumble! Such things must come, but woe to the person through whom they come!" (NIV).

Again, in Luke 17:1, we read: "Jesus said to his disciples: 'Things that cause people to stumble are bound to come, but woe to anyone through whom they come.'" (NIV).

We notice from these scriptures that hurts and offences will come, but woe to those who perpetrate them. The one who offends or hurts you and refuses to take note and do the right thing has an answer to give to the Lord someday, so why don't you leave the offender to the Lord to deal with and get on with your life? It is a fearful thing to fall into the hands of the Lord, and he says vengeance is his. It is not an easy thing to forgive, but it is possible. There are a lot of us who go to church, but the word of God has very little impact on our lives. What we hear and do are two different things.

Jesus gave an illustration in Matthew 13:20–21, and part of it reads: "The seeds that fell on rocky ground stands for those who receive the message gladly as soon as they hear it. But it does not sink into them, and they don't last long. So when trouble or persecution comes because of the message, they give up at once." (GNT)

I suppose you don't want to be like the seed that fell on the rocky places and had no root. In your hurting moments and circumstances, what do you do with the word that you have been hearing all this while? In times like this, you need the help of the Holy Spirit. The word may even vanish from you. All you can remember may be the hurt or offence.

Many people have left the church and found themselves as "Lone Ranger Christians"—LRCs. This usually happens because of offences and hurts that they have suffered in the church. Some people have been seriously maligned, libelled, and scandalized in church, and they wonder and ask themselves, where am I? Am I dealing with Christians or unbelievers? Hello! Is anybody listening? People have quit church because of false accusations, harassment, gossip, and indiscretions on the part of pastors or prophets and others involved in the church. Others have also quit just because they were disciplined for wrong behaviours. If all this is happening in the church, what about the people out there who do not know the Lord or care a hoot about him? It will surprise you to know that sometimes the people outside the church may be better in terms of good deeds. This is sad, but it is true.

Hurts and offences are destroying and weakening the church and individuals. They are eating the unity, strength, and power of the church away. One of the reasons the anointing is sometimes not felt in the church is that there is so much bitterness around. When people jostle for positions in the church as if they are in a political contest, people usually become bitter. I have seen the machete scars of a would-be head of a church just before church elections. Why on earth should this happen in the body of Christ? Pastors and pastors' wives are hurting and offending each other and creating foul atmospheres in the church. The sad aspect is that we refuse to acknowledge our mistakes and apologize to one another because of pride, which is the nature of the devil anyway. Unforgiveness is very much alive in this kind of situation, and the funny side of it is that these men and women of God will meet in church and will not talk to each other; they will pass by and not greet each other. They always look in the opposite direction as if the other does not exist. After that they stand in front of the congregation and say big things as if they have just landed from heaven. Sometimes it is amazing how church members are able to read through all these funny behaviours. It's sad, to say the least. It affects the spirituality of the church. The Holy Spirit is grieved and hindered in his work in such an environment.

Families, organizations, and groups are also breaking up or being fragmented as a result of hurts and offences. Jesus one day told his disciples that, because of him, they would be offended and fall away: "Then Jesus told them, 'This very night you will all fall away on account of me, for it is written: I will strike the shepherd, and the sheep of the flock will be scattered'" (Matthew 26:31 NIV). "Blessed is the man who does not stumble on account of me" (Matthew 11:6 NIV).

Jesus's disciples deserted him in the face of persecution, and yet he was not offended. The people of his hometown disregarded him and looked down upon him, and, I am sure, said all sorts of things about him.

Can you believe that somebody stopped going to church because he was not being shown "respect" as an important person in society? There was a bishop who used to attend programmes in another church. Whenever he went into the meeting, he would sit at the back until, one day, an usher drew the attention of the general overseer to this practice. This bishop has churches all over the world, but never demanded that he should be given a seat in front. He was never offended by where he sat to worship. There are some church members who will not come to church again if a stranger should make the mistake of occupying their "usual seats." They will be offended and unforgiving. The Pharisees were offended by Jesus's teachings and popularity. They could not forgive him for taking all their church members, but I don't remember anywhere in the Bible that tells us that Jesus apologized for this. Their thinking and interpretations of the work of the Lord were totally wrong. It is clear from the foregoing that sometimes we are offended or hurt by our own thinking and evil interpretations just like the Pharisees. Are you offended just because what you heard is not favourable to you, even though it is the truth? Don't sin because of the truth.

Saul, who was later called Paul, became very offended when John Mark deserted him and Barnabas on their first missionary trip; however, in due course he had to change his mind and accept to work with him again. He had every reason to remain offended; however, he forgave and changed his mind. We should be able to do as Jesus did by not falling away on account of somebody's action or inaction and, like Paul, be able to let go when offended. They did not remain in bitterness. When we stand before God in judgment, it will not be on account of who did what to us, it will be what we did or our reaction in that situation in relation to the word of God.

> Coming to his hometown, he began teaching the people in their synagogue, and they were amazed. "Where did this man get this wisdom and these miraculous powers?" they asked. "Isn't this the carpenter's son? Isn't his mother's name Mary, and aren't his brothers James, Joseph, Simon and Judas? Aren't all his sisters with us? Where then did this man get all

these things?" And they took offense at him.
(Matthew 13:54–57 NIV)

There are some people who have been offended as a result
of their pride or egos being punctured. This could be because
God may be using somebody in the church, in the family, or
even at the workplace instead of them. There have been many
instances in which choir members, especially, have fallen prey
to this kind of evil tactics of the devil. Many churches can testify
to this. When someone is chosen to be a lead singer instead of
you, even though you may be a better singer, how do you react?
If you are offended because God has promoted somebody above
you, then you'd better check yourself. You are not ready for ele-
vation. I have been there before. I thought I was more quali-
fied to lead a certain Christian fellowship when the executives
decided someone else should lead. It took grace for me to continue in fellowship. It hurt so much, but I had to "grow up" and
let go of my pain and anger. To be frank with you, it was a real
struggle. If you find yourself in this kind of situation, where you
are not ready to let go, you may either be suffering from pride,
low self-esteem, or just immaturity. This is what happened to
Cain when God accepted Abel's offering but rejected his. He
became angry and offended.

In Genesis 4:2–8 we are told:

> Now Abel kept flocks, and Cain worked the
> soil. In the course of time Cain brought some of
> the fruits of the soil as an offering to the Lord.
> But Abel brought fat portions from some of
> the firstborn of his flock. The Lord looked with
> favor on Abel and his offering, but on Cain and
> his offering he did not look with favor. So Cain
> was very angry, and his face was downcast.

> Then the Lord said to Cain, "Why are you angry? Why is your face downcast? If you do what is right, will you not be accepted? But if you do not do what is right, sin is crouching at your door; it desires to have you, but you must master it."
>
> Now Cain said to his brother Abel, "Let's go out to the field." And while they were in the field, Cain attacked his brother Abel and killed him. (NIV)

Cain couldn't forgive God or his brother and therefore planned revenge. That is why he invited Abel out into the field where he murdered him. Hurt and offence can lead to bitterness and to murder.

The people of Jesus's hometown could not accept what Jesus was doing because, I believe, some of them were thinking they were better off than this carpenter's son whose family had no pedigree. They were from known families with all sorts of credentials. Who does this carpenter's son think he is? They were thus offended by his popularity and exploits. Because of the attitude of the people, the Bible says, Jesus could not do many miracles in his hometown. Offence will rob you of your blessings. I am telling you this as Jesus told his disciples in John 16:1, which reads, "All this I have told you so that you will not go astray" (NIV). So you will also not go astray into bitterness from your latent simmering anger or pain.

This is one example of what an offender can do without batting an eye and getting away with it:

"Which way did he go when he left?" the old prophet asked them. They showed him the road and he told them to saddle his donkey for him. They did so, and he rode off down the road after the prophet from Judah and found him sitting under an oak tree. "Are you the prophet from Judah?" he asked.

"I am," the man answered.

"Come home and have a meal with me," he said.

But the prophet from Judah answered, "I can't go home with you or accept your hospitality. And I won't eat or drink anything with you here, because the Lord has commanded me not to eat or drink a thing, and not to return home the same way I came."

Then the old prophet from Bethel said to him, "I, too, am a prophet just like you, and at the Lord's command an angel told me to take you home with me and offer you my hospitality." But the old prophet was lying.

So the prophet from Judah went home with the old prophet and had a meal with him. As they were sitting at the table, the word of the Lord came to the old prophet, and he cried out to the prophet from Judah, "The Lord says that you disobeyed him and did not do what he commanded. Instead, you returned and ate a meal in a place he had ordered you not to eat in. Because of this you will be killed, and your body will not be buried in your family grave."

After they had finished eating, the old prophet saddled the donkey for the prophet from Judah, who rode off. On the way a lion met him and killed him. His body lay on the road, and the donkey and the lion stood beside it. Some men passed by and saw the body on the road, with the lion standing nearby. They went on

into Bethel and reported what they had seen.
(1 Kings 13:12–25 GNT)

In this story, an old prophet lies to a younger one whom God had sent to the king of Judah with specific instructions. This young prophet obeyed God to a certain extent and then, as a result of deception (offence) by the old prophet, he disobeyed God. The result was disastrous for the one who was deceived and induced to disobey. He paid the ultimate price with his life while the offender lived on. Why did God not kill the offender too? If I were to act on behalf of God, justice would have demanded the life of the old prophet too. If God could allow the offender to go "scot-free" (which is difficult to accept), who are you to allow hurts and offences to grow into bitterness in your life? The fact that you cannot understand some of these actions of God does not give you the license to take matters into your own hands. Bitterness is sin, and the wages of sin can be only "death." Don't die a useless death while the offenders enjoy their lives. Jesus said in John 15:18, "If the world hates you, keep in mind that it hated me first." (NIV)

I hope you are not thinking that this writer is an angel from heaven who has fallen through the clouds and therefore is not in tune with reality. This writer is just like anybody else who has gone through some experiences that made him bitter, but by the grace of God was delivered from that bondage of bitterness. Let me give you an example. This writer signed a vehicle hire purchase agreement with a certain man, and this agreement was guaranteed by someone he knew. This person messed up the vehicle, stole about three months' sales equivalent (quite an amount), and disappeared. I was so hurt and offended that I even attempted taking him to court, but at a point in time, I had to let go for Christ's sake. I looked at the state of the man and realized that there was no way he could pay back what he had misappropriated. It was not easy! I took my car back and spent more money to repair it. He really had made a mess of my car. Friend, there are times you have to pay this kind of price for the sake of the kingdom. Yes, you may have to! Actually, some people thought my decision to let go was not right because the guy never learnt anything good from the encounter. However, don't let your hurts and offences rob you of your blessings. Sometimes these things also come as trials, which we will discuss in the next chapter.

Chapter 3

SUFFERINGS AND TRIALS

Sufferings and trials are part and parcel of human life. They are also the cause of bitterness for some people. When you are suffering and facing trials, there is always the tendency to become angry and bitter, especially when you cannot see the end of your troubles. I don't know of any human being who takes delight in suffering, who wakes up in the morning and prays for trials and pain throughout the day. I don't! But the fact that you don't ask for it does not mean it will not come. It will. However, the most important issue here is what you do in the face of your sufferings. This is why I tend to agree with Henri J. M. Nouwen when he says:

> We fail to see the place of suffering in the broader scheme of things. We fail to see that suffering is an inevitable dimension of life. Because we have lost perspective, we fail to see that unless one is willing to accept suffering properly, he or she is really refusing to continue

in the quest for maturity. To refuse suffering is
to refuse personal growth.[5]

Refusal to accept suffering as part of life has caused many
to miss certain vital lessons in life.

Terrible things happen to both good and bad people. Have
you ever come to that place where you believe you have done
everything right, serving God to the best of your ability, doing
good to people, working hard at your job, and yet your sufferings and trials don't seem to end? You have prayed and asked
God all the questions you could think of, but there is no answer,
and your problems keep on mounting.

Many people, especially Christians, have become bitter
today because they believe God has disappointed them. Some
are suffering from incurable diseases, some are being mistreated
by husbands or fathers, some own businesses that are on the
verge of collapse for no apparent reason. You may have failed
your exams after studying hard and praying, your church or fellowship may be collapsing even though you have God's assurance that it is well but it is not well with you. Perhaps you have
lost a child, and it looks as if God does not care anymore. You
work so hard and yet poverty is like a tight-fitting diving suit
on you. You have been married for some time now but have no
child, and your in-laws are not giving you any peace. As a pastor, you have been praying for people who have been testifying
in church as to what God is doing for them, but you are not having your breakthrough. It is as if your name is "Berko" (a hustler
or struggler). Your pain and sufferings know no end.

When people suffer for a long time without any hope of getting out of their problems, they become disgruntled, bitter, and
sometimes resigned to whatever has overtaken them. For two
years Absalom suffered so much internal pain and external disgrace that, at a certain point in time, he had to let out his suffering

in explosive anger. Tamar, Absalom's sister, suffered greatly from shame and disgrace and had to live as a desolate woman all her life whilst Amnon, the one who defiled her, continued to live his princely life. What was her heart like? I wish I could tell.

Early on, I made a statement that the most important issue about suffering and trials is your reaction, and I want to illustrate that thought with this story. There was a young Christian couple who lived in a war-torn country and had been married for about eight years without a child. In their ninth year together, God blessed them with twins, and they had another child a year later. When the twins were about two years old, they both died mysteriously from a strange disease, and this devastated the couple. Their faith was greatly shaken. The woman in particular could not take it. She could not understand why God had not intervened or prevented the deaths. Her conclusion was that serving God was a useless venture. She was so bitter with God that she did not care about him anymore. Whether he existed or not was none of her business. She began to care less about the other child and the husband, because if God did not care, why should she? God could go ahead and do whatever he liked. She could not be bothered. She was too bitter to endure and to think through what she could do positively in her suffering. She gave up on life and, in no time, became depressed and an alcoholic.

One of the most difficult things about Christianity is the fact that becoming a child of God does not make you an untouchable so far as sufferings and trials are concerned, but thank God for Romans 8:28: "And we know that in all things God works for the good of those who love him, who have been called according to his purpose." This tells me that God has a reason for allowing us to go through all the sufferings and trials we go through. My prayer is that God will help you in your sufferings to know and understand his purpose in what is going on. It is not easy to do this. You need the fellowship of the Holy Spirit to help you. There are times that we just refuse to understand, depending on the severity of the suffering; nevertheless, it does not change the purpose of God.

Apart from Jesus there are these three people in the Bible who suffered so much and faced all kinds of trials, not because of their sins, but rather to fulfil the purpose of God for their lives. They are Joseph, Job, and Daniel. Joseph did not do anything wrong to deserve the treatment his brothers gave him or for God to allow him to go through what he went through—the pit, slavery, and imprisonment, but all was to fulfil God's agenda as stated in Genesis 45:4–7:

> Then Joseph said to his brothers, "Come close to me." When they had done so, he said, "I am your brother Joseph, the one you sold into Egypt! And now, do not be distressed and do not be angry with yourselves for selling me here, because it was to save lives that God sent me ahead of you. For two years now there has been famine in the land, and for the next five years there will not be plowing and reaping. *But God sent me ahead of you to preserve for you a remnant on earth and to save your lives by a great deliverance.* (NIV, emphasis mine)

What did Job do wrong? His only "crime" was that God boasted about him and permitted the devil to test him. In the end—in spite of Job's suffering—God's purpose was achieved. If Job had been angry and bitter all this while and had even gone ahead to curse God and died as suggested by the wife (due to his sufferings), I don't know what his end would have looked like. Looking at the terrible things these people went through, I believe that if the same things had happened to some of us Christians of today, we would have heaped all the blame on

God, who is an easy target for us in times of crises. Sometimes it is very difficult to understand God's standards and his way of doing things, and so at this point I believe it would not be out of place if one should ask, "Why does God allow his children to go through all the sufferings and trials of life?" Let's take a look at the story of a certain woman in the Bible called Naomi, and her daughter-in-law. It may help us understand God a little:

> "Don't call me Naomi," she told them. "Call me Mara, because the Almighty has made my life very bitter. I went away full, but the Lord has brought me back empty. Why call me Naomi? The Lord has afflicted me; the Almighty has brought misfortune upon me." (Ruth 1:20– 21 NIV)

Naomi attributed all her misfortunes to God because, in those days, they believed that God was all powerful and everything came from him. We see here that God used the misfortunes of Naomi to bring blessings to her and her daughter-in-law, Ruth, who later became an ancestor of the Messiah. Incredible!

> Then Naomi took the child in her arms and cared for him. The women living there said, "Naomi has a son." And they named him Obed. He was the father of Jesse, the father of David. (Ruth 4:16–17 NIV)

God used the suffering of Ruth and Naomi to fulfil his own purpose.

> And the God of all grace, who called you to his eternal glory in Christ, after you have suffered a little while, will himself restore you and make you strong, firm and steadfast. (1 Peter 5:10 NIV)

This is an encouraging scripture to help you hold on a little while till you see the salvation of the Lord. It may keep you from growing bitter. Let me encourage you that the suffering is for a while; it is not permanent.

In some parts of Africa, and Ghana in particular, it is not unusual for a person to be the forty-fifth child of his father and the first of his mother. In that sort of family, which is most of the time poverty ridden, this forty-fifth child will not be alien to suffering and love deficiency. Such a child will have no love relation with the father, and is likely to live in misery. How can such a person forgive his father and get rid of bitterness?

Recently I heard an account on the radio of a little boy of about seven years old whose mother sold him to a fisherman for about a quarter of that country's current basic monthly salary. I will not be able to recount all the harrowing experiences of this little boy in this chapter, but let me tell you one. One day the master and some other children went on a fishing expedition. When they returned to the bank, they realized that the net they had been using was entangled and could not be dragged to the banks of the river. One of the little boys was asked to dive into the water and disentangle the net. He came back and reported that he could not disentangle the net. A very sharp rebuke and threats from the master sent him running back into the water, but he never returned. When this boy's dead body was retrieved from the river, it was in such a horrible state that the master himself attempted to commit suicide, and the effect it had on this boy I'm talking about was unimaginable. How could this boy ever forgive his mother for all the horrible things he experienced?

Why do we suffer sometimes?

1. One of the reasons we suffer, I believe, is to draw us closer to God and enable us to depend on his grace and power on a daily basis. Paul, the great apostle, had a problem. He prayed to God for deliverance, but all God told him was, "my grace is sufficient for you, for my power is made perfect in weakness." That is why Paul could say that he delighted in his weakness, for when he was weak, then he was strong. What a grace! We need this kind of grace to help us to stand firm and not fall into bitterness in times of suffering. Focusing on the grace available helps to stop us from sliding into bitternes.

   > To keep me from becoming conceited because of these surpassingly great revelations, there was given me a thorn in my flesh, a messenger of Satan, to torment me. Three times I pleaded with the Lord to take it away from me. But he said to me, "My grace is sufficient for you, for my power is made perfect in weakness." Therefore, I will boast all the more gladly about my weaknesses, so that Christ's power may rest on me. That is why, for Christ's sake, I delight in weaknesses, in insults, in hardships, in persecutions, in difficulties. For when I am weak, then I am strong. (2 Corinthians 12:7–10 NIV)

2. Suffering helps us to produce the fruit of the spirit, which is the nature and character of Christ.

   > Not only so, but we also rejoice in our sufferings, because we know that suffering produces perseverance; perseverance, character; and character, hope. (Romans 5:3–4 NIV)

> Consider it pure joy, my brothers, whenever you face trials of many kinds, because you know that the testing of your faith develops perseverance. Perseverance must finish its work so that you may be mature and complete, not lacking anything. (James 1:2–5 NIV)

> Suffering is a kind of pruning which God does to help us bear more fruit. Pruning is not a pleasant thing; however, it is necessary for every child of God to go through occasionally. Without pruning, you will not bear much fruit, and the fruit will not be the best quality (John 15:1–2).

3. God uses suffering to teach, train, and mature us to be like Christ. Imagine having a child who has no idea about suffering. Can this child take care of any inheritance you leave for him or her? Many empires have failed because the inheritors had no idea of the price that was paid for its establishment. Do you remember Rehoboam who inherited from his father Solomon? He never suffered for anything and therefore could afford to joke with the kingdom and make useless decisions that never helped the cause of the dynasty.

> Before I was afflicted I went astray, but now I obey your word. (Psalm 119:67 NIV)

> It was good for me to be afflicted so that I might learn your decrees. (Psalm 119:71 NIV)

> In this you greatly rejoice, though now for a little while you may have had to suffer grief in all kinds of trials. These have come so that your faith—of greater worth than gold, which perishes even

though refined by fire—may be proved genuine and may result in praise, glory and honor when Jesus Christ is revealed. (1 Peter 1:6–7 NIV)

Moreover, we have all had human fathers who disciplined us and we respected them for it. How much more should we submit to the Father of our spirits and live! Our fathers disciplined us for a little while as they thought best; but God disciplines us for our good, that we may share in his holiness. (Hebrews 12:9–10 NIV)

Dear friends, do not be surprised at the painful trial you are suffering, as though something strange were happening to you. 13 But rejoice that you participate in the sufferings of Christ, so that you may be overjoyed when his glory is revealed. (1 Peter 4:12–13 NIV)

I want to know Christ and the power of his resurrection and the fellowship of sharing in his sufferings. (Philippians 3:10 NIV)

But we have this treasure in jars of clay to show that this all-surpassing power is from God and not from us. We are hard pressed on every side, but not crushed; perplexed, but not in despair; persecuted, but not abandoned; struck down, but not destroyed. (2 Corinthians 4:7–9 NIV)

All these scriptures tell you that your suffering is not for nothing. It is definitely for a purpose. I must say here that, at the time of suffering, it is not easy to sit down and find out from God the purpose of what you are going through, but you need to do so; otherwise, you will focus so much on your suffering that you might even forget that God exists. You will need the help of the Holy Spirit to be able to focus on God and not your condition at this time. He is our helper.

4. When you are matured in Christ through suffering, you become an example or role model, a counsellor, an advisor, and an encourager. You build the capacity to empathize and help. A man of God that I admire so much lost two daughters in an accident. Even though he grieved so much his pain did not make him bitter against God it rather drew him closer.

> Simon, Simon, Satan has asked to sift you as wheat. But I have prayed for you, Simon that your faith may not fail. And when you have turned back, strengthen your brothers. (Luke 22:31–32 NIV)

> Praise be to the God and Father of our Lord Jesus Christ, the Father of compassion and the God of all comfort, who comforts us in all our troubles, so that we can comfort those in any trouble with the comfort we ourselves have received from God. (2 Corinthians 1:3–4 NIV)

> You became imitators of us and of the Lord; in spite of severe suffering, you welcomed the message with the joy given by the Holy Spirit. And so you became a model to all the believers in Macedonia and Achaia. (Thessalonians 1 1:6–7 NIV)

To this you were called, because Christ suffered for you, leaving you an example that you should follow in his steps. (1 Peter 2:21 NIV)

Christ himself was an example to us in suffering. Are you a model to the believers as a result of your sufferings and trials, or just one of the bitter persons around making the numbers? May God help us.

5.   Suffering helps to manifest the power of God and to glorify him.

And call upon me in the day of trouble; I will deliver you, and you will honor me. (Psalm 50:15 NIV)

As he went along, he saw a man blind from birth. His disciples asked him, "Rabbi, who sinned, this man or his parents, that he was born blind?" "Neither this man nor his parents sinned," said Jesus, "but this happened so that the work of God might be displayed in his life." (John 9: 1–3 NIV)

For I know that through your prayers and the help given by the Spirit of Jesus Christ, what has happened to me will turn out for my deliverance. I eagerly expect and hope that I will in no way be ashamed, but will have sufficient courage so that now as always Christ will be exalted in my body, whether by life or by death. (Philippians 1:19–20 NIV)

God's name is glorified when you go through your suffering and come out still holding on to your faith. Your testimony brings glory to the father and overcomes the enemy (Revelation 12:11 NIV).

6. God chastens his children; therefore, suffering sometimes proves that we are children of God. It is not every kind of suffering that proves our sonship. Stealing and living the life of a robber and a vagabond and suffering for this behaviour does not indicate that you are a child of God. Until you come to Christ and abandon your old nature, your suffering shows something else.

> And you have forgotten that word of encouragement that addresses you as sons: "My son, do not make light of the Lord's discipline, and do not lose heart when he rebukes you, because the Lord disciplines those he loves, and he punishes everyone he accepts as a son. (Hebrews 12:5–6 NIV)

> You will not be a real child if the father never rebukes or punishes you for anything. A child who never gets punished for wrong things is not loved.

7. Suffering can reveal who we really are on the inside. Our real character is revealed when we are under pressure. How do you behave when you are suffering or under any form of pressure? Do you curse, insult, break rules, and pay bribes? Or do you seek help from above? Trials develop character.

Therefore I despise myself and repent in dust and ashes. (Job 42:6–7 NIV)

I will set out and go back to my father and say to him: Father, I have sinned against heaven and against you. (Luke 15:18 NIV)

You come out a better person after your trials and sufferings because you can learn to trust God more, become more patient, and learn to persevere.

8. Suffering sometimes deals with pride in our lives and prevents us from living in sin.

    To keep me from becoming conceited because of these surpassingly great revelations, there was given me a thorn in my flesh, a messenger of Satan, to torment me. Three times I pleaded with the Lord to take it away from me. But he said to me, "My grace is sufficient for you, for my power is made perfect in weakness." Therefore, I will boast all the more gladly about my weaknesses, so that Christ's power may rest on me. That is why, for Christ's sake, I delight in weaknesses, in insults, in hardships, in persecutions, in difficulties. For when I am weak, then I am strong. (2 Corinthians 12:7– 10 NIV)

9. Suffering helps to prepare us for greater or higher ministry work and any other expansion that God, in his wisdom and grace, may bring our way.

    I tell you the truth unless a kernel of wheat falls to the ground and dies, it remains only a single seed. But if it dies, it produces many seeds. (John 12:24–25 NIV)

Falling into the ground and dying is not child's play. It means suffering, and it is a price one must pay to handle great things for God. Examples of this abound in the Bible.

If you want to know the truth in this, find out from any of the great men of God you know. You will be surprised by what they have gone through or are going through. Greatness does not come cheap.

10. Suffering opens our eyes to see and understand the nature and sovereignty of God. He does what he likes at any time. You cannot question and disagree with him. Being bitter somehow questions the sovereignty of God. Even if you question him, it must not be about his integrity.

For you, O God, tested us; you refined us like silver. You brought us into prison and laid burdens on our backs. You let men ride over our heads; we went through fire and water, but you brought us to a place of abundance. (Psalm 66:10–12 NIV)

11. Suffering is of a short duration and not comparable to what blessings awaits us in heaven. It is for a season and it will surely come to pass. It has an expiry date, check it!

And the God of all grace, who called you to his eternal glory in Christ, after you have suffered a little while, will himself restore you and make you strong, firm and steadfast. (1 Peter 5:10 NIV)

I consider that our present sufferings are not worth comparing with the glory that will be revealed in us. The creation waits in eager expectation for the sons of God to be revealed. (Romans 8:18–19 NIV)

But rejoice that you participate in the sufferings of Christ, so that you may be overjoyed when his glory is revealed. (1 Peter 4:13 NIV)

And we know that in all things God works for the good of those who love him, who are called according to his purpose. (Romans 8:28 NIV)

Consider it pure joy, my brothers, whenever you face trials on many kinds, because you know that the testing of your faith develops perseverance. Perseverance must finish its work so that you may be mature and complete, not lacking any thing. Blessed is the man who perseveres under trial, because when he has stood the test, he will receive the crown of life that God has promised to thos who love him. (James 1:2–4, 12 NIV)

Many a time we blame our sufferings and trials on Satan, demons, witches, the old ladies in our hometown or the area where we live, and other people we consider as enemies. These entities cannot be fully absolved from blame, but you can see from the reasons mentioned early on that sometimes God allows these things to happen to us for a reason. I read the story of a young man in a certain country who was suffering in life. He went to consult a fetish priest who told him that his grandmother was a witch and was using her witchcraft to cause all his problems. The young man did not take kindly to this "revelation." He went home and butchered the old lady to death. He was arrested, and he landed in prison with a death sentence hanging on his neck.

A lot of people who are suffering and facing all kinds of trials may not end up in physical prison like this young man, but spiritually they will be in emotional and mental prisons. They will become so bitter that they will not be free in themselves. They will become bitter in the sense that they will be unable to forgive the person or persons who caused their sufferings, especially when such sufferings persist for a long time. In Africa most of the sufferings people go through are attributed to somebody.

We sometimes suffer not because of something we have done wrong; however, it pays to do a self-examination to be sure of that. Could it be something ancestral? You have the power to break the cycle as a child of God. You should not allow yourself to sink into bitterness and destroy your life.

Have you ever considered why Joseph (the son of Jacob), Job, Shadrach, Meshach, Abednego, Daniel, Paul, and all the apostles had to go through everything that happened to them? What would you have done if you were in their shoes? Joseph, for instance, did not keep any hateful and evil thoughts as a result of what he suffered.

Continue to believe in God despite the fact that you don't understand his ways, especially during times of suffering and trials. Know that his ways are not our ways; neither are his thoughts.

> "For my thoughts are not your thoughts, neither are your ways my ways," declares the Lord. "As the heavens are higher than the earth, so are my ways higher than your ways and my thoughts than your thoughts." (Isaiah 55:8–9 NIV)

Focus on your God and his plan for your life and keep rejoicing in him. It is important to check our thoughts when we go through suffering so that we do not become bitter through hateful and bitter thoughts.

> Though the fig tree does not bud and there are
> no grapes on the vines, though the olive crop fails
> and the fields produce no food, though there are
> no sheep in the pen and no cattle   in the stalls,
> yet I will rejoice in the Lord, I will be joyful in
> God my Savior. (Habakkuk 3:17– 18 NIV)

Hold on when you can't see the end of trouble. Hold on when you cannot hear God's still, small voice. And hold on when you do not feel as if God is there at all. David Michael Lee wrote, "The lesson learned for all of us is that God is holding on to us even when we don't feel his arms around us."[6]

Chapter 4

HATEFUL AND EVIL THOUGHTS

You will always become bitter when you maintain a "disciplined" life of hatred and evil thoughts. Or is it because you will be forced to deal with the pain of letting go, as American writer James Arthur Baldwin says, "I imagine one of the reasons people cling to their hates so stubbornly is because they sense once hate is gone … they will be forced to deal with pain."[7] Dealing with pain may not be an easy thing to handle, so to avoid any difficulties a person may choose to hold on to hatred. But according to the early Greek poet Hesoid, "He harms himself who does evil to another, and the evil plan is most harmful to the planner."[8] Why will you do this to yourself?

How can you forgive somebody you hate on a daily basis? You cannot incubate hatred and evil thoughts without giving birth to bitterness. Can a person take hot burning coals into his or her lap without being burned? The fear of having to deal with your pain may truly cause you to hate the source, and this may also lead you to evil plans that will, in the end, affect you negatively. Absalom, the son of King David, is a true reflection of the two quotations above. He was full of hatred and evil thoughts, and in the end, he destroyed himself. Should we say the devil destroyed him? Hatred and evil thoughts are entrenched by unforgiveness. In so far as you refuse to forgive, you can never cease to have hateful and evil thoughts. It is impossible.

Hatred is a strong emotion of intense dislike. It very often causes people to take action. The story of Absalom confirms this definition. Absalom's feeling of dislike for his half-brother, Ammon, was so strong that he felt the need to take action to let out all the venom that had been festering all the while. This illustrates a further definition of hatred as a feeling of deep hostility against a person or thing.

Evil thoughts and evil plans may result in evil actions. We notice here that the underlying factor for hateful and evil thoughts is unforgiveness. Let's examine another example of what hatred and evil thoughts can do: "For John had been saying to Herod, 'It is unlawful for you to have your brother's wife.' So Herodias nursed a grudge against John and wanted to kill him. But she was not able to" (Mark 6:18–19 NIV)

Looking at the definitions of hatred I've just discussed, it is evidently clear that Herodias harboured an extreme anger and bore a grudge against John the Baptist for a long time. She nursed such hateful and evil thoughts that she even wanted to kill him. She hated him until the day she got the opportunity to pour out her bitterness by having him executed. Because she hated him, I am inclined to believe that all her thoughts about this man were evil through and through. I wonder if it is possible to think well about someone you hate so much. That is why she did not have to think twice or blink an eye in asking for the head of John the Baptist when the opportunity came. Those hateful and evil thoughts had taken root to become bitterness. Have you noticed that it is not easy to keep good thoughts when there is hatred in your heart? When you hate somebody you easily become aggravated by the person's behaviour or attitude, even sometimes his or her looks are a problem for you. You can hardly be yourself in the presence of this person and even get agitated by thinking of him or her. You sometimes become intolerant, argumentative, antagonistic, confrontational, and sometimes aggressive towards the person. With this kind of mind, why wouldn't you think maliciously or even have fantasies of murdering this person? You grow cold and even become enraged when you hear the name of the person. Some will even not take the same route that the so-called enemy took though they may be going to the same place. You have a problem. The root of bitterness is in you and you have to do something about it.

Another example of the effects of hateful and evil thoughts can be found in the story of Shimei and King David as told in 2 Samuel:

Shimei Curses David

As King David came to Bahurim, a man came out of the village cursing them. It was Shimei son of Gera, from the same clan as Saul's family. He threw stones at the king and the king's officers and all the mighty warriors who surrounded him. "Get out of here, you murderer, you scoundrel!" he shouted at David. "The Lord is paying you back for all the bloodshed in Saul's clan. You stole his throne, and now the Lord has given it to your son Absalom. At last you will taste some of your own medicine, for you are a murderer!"

"Why should this dead dog curse my lord the king?" Abishai son of Zeruiah demanded. "Let me go over and cut off his head!"

"No!" the king said. "Who asked your opinion, you sons of Zeruiah! If the Lord has told him to curse me, who are you to stop him?"

Then David said to Abishai and to all his servants, "My own son is trying to kill me. Doesn't this relative of Saul have even more reason to do so? Leave him alone and let him curse, for the Lord has told him to do it. And perhaps the Lord will see that I am being wronged and will bless me because of these curses today." So David and his men continued down the road, and Shimei kept pace with them on a nearby hillside, cursing and throwing stones and dirt at David.

The king and all who were with him grew weary along the way, so they rested when they reached the Jordan River. (2 Samuel 16:5– 14 NLT)

From this story, it would not be farfetched to believe that Shimei, all the while that David was king, bore a grudge against him because he always thought that it was David who killed Saul and his family. Saul had been dead for over twenty years, but Shimei still harboured these sentiments and never forgave David because of his understanding of the issues. He nurtured this evil of bitterness throughout the years just as Absalom did. He said, "The Lord has repaid you for all the blood you shed in the household of Saul, in whose place you have reigned." (2 Samuel 16:8 NIV). Shimei was evidently bitter against David, which never showed up until the day that David lost power and had to go into exile. It is important to note here that sometimes the premise upon which people become bitter can be very wrong, just as it was in the case of Shimei. It is also a wicked thing for a person to rejoice over the predicaments of another out of bitterness, especially if that person is a child of God. God will definitely take note. A clear example can be found in Ezekiel 25:1–7. The Ammonites rejoiced over the predicaments of Judah, and as a result, God pronounced serious judgement on them.

Sometimes the basis of the hatred may be just hearsay or rumour, which has not been proven anywhere. I have seen and heard about fights breaking out among tenants living in a "compound house" just because someone had been told that another person was gossiping about him or her. Without any proof whatsoever, the offended attacks the so-called offender, and a chaotic scene breaks out. There are so many scriptures in the Bible that prove that David never had a hand in the death of Saul, and one of them can be found in the story below.

> But David said to Abishai, "Don't destroy him! Who can lay a hand on the Lord's anointed and be guiltless? As surely as the Lord lives," he said, "the Lord himself will strike him; either his time will come and he will die, or he will go into battle and perish. But the Lord forbid that I should lay a hand on the Lord's anointed. Now get the spear and water jug that are near his head, and let's go."

> So David took the spear and water jug near Saul's head, and they left. No one saw or knew about it, nor did anyone wake up. They were all sleeping, because the Lord had put them into a deep sleep. (1 Samuel 26:9–12 NIV)

Let us look at more causes of hateful and evil thoughts.

1. Controlling and domineering authority. Have you ever had a domineering, controlling boss, spouse, parent, sibling, friend, co-worker, or neighbour? How does it feel? When someone tries to control or manipulate your life, just because he or she has the power to do so and try to make life difficult for you, the natural thing is for you to be angry and resentful. This is one of the reasons that teenagers rebel against their parents and other people in authority. Sometimes when someone feels incapable of facing up to a "superior," he or she begins to hate that person, especially when life is generally unbearable under that entity. If you have someone in your life who is a bully and does not like you, you are likely to fall under this condition.

    When you bring this into the church situation and you have one person wanting to be the leader of everything, scheming all the time to unseat others, the person's actions create an atmosphere for hateful and evil thoughts. This does not augur well for the spirituality of the church.

2. Abandonment and betrayal. Every human being, at one point in time or the other, has put his or her trust and faith in one person or another; for example, husband and wife put their trust and faith in each other. When this trust is betrayed in any form, the one who is betrayed may begin to hate the other, and where there is no apology and forgiveness, bitterness sets in. Abandonment and cheating, especially in marriage, can cause severe hatred. There are couples who are in relationships and yet hate their spouses for some of these reasons. Have you ever been betrayed by a very trusted spouse, friend, business partner, or an immediate supervisor? What about your pastor or a

church elder? These situations I must say are not very easy to handle. It takes time and much prayer to get over them.

3.   Exposure of failures or shortcomings. There are also some people who become offended and angry when their failures or shortcomings are pointed out to them, no matter how it is done. Sometimes this kind of attitude is as a result of pride. How do you feel when your reputation or integrity is attacked for no apparent reason, or you never receive approval or recognition for who you are and all the good things you think you do?

4.   Comparison. You may be a young person who is always being compared to other people, especially other siblings, but never recognized for your unique personality. This could be very disturbing. You may either hate yourself or the person who is doing this to you or possibly the one you are compared with.

5.   Disappointments. In Africa, and I believe in many cultures all over the world, the future of the young ones or many family members is dependent on one or two bread winners in the family. When providers act in any way which negatively affects the future of the dependents, the likelihood of some of the dependents hating them is very high. I know of a situation in which the father in the family was very rich, but due to his insatiable lust for women and alcohol, he lost all his riches and therefore jeopardized the education of his children. They never had an easy life and found it difficult to forgive this man. They always cursed him for making their lives so miserable.

6.   Insubordination. Another cause of hatred is insubordination and unwillingness on the part of a junior or a subordinate to submit to control, guidance, or authority. This happens especially between young adults and their parents and sometimes in the office setting.

7.   Jealousy. There is something called *ahoɔyaa* in Ghana. It literally means "skin pain." It borders on jealousy and hatred. Sometimes this situation arises when others succeed where we have failed and seem to have an easy life while we struggle. Typical examples can be found in the Bible between Saul and David, and Jesus and the religious authorities of his time:

> When the men were returning home after David had killed the Philistine, the women came out from all the towns of Israel to meet King Saul with singing and dancing, with joyful songs and with tambourines and lutes. As they danced, they sang: "Saul has slain his thousands, and David his tens of thousands."
>
> Saul was very angry; this refrain galled him. "They have credited David with tens of thousands," he thought, "but me with only thousands. What more can he get but the kingdom?" And from that time on Saul kept a jealous eye on David. (1 Samuel 18:6–9 NIV)

King Saul and the whole of Israel were afraid of Goliath, the Philistine champion who had defied the armies of Israel. For several days, this giant soldier challenged the armies of Israel on the battlefield, and no one could take him on until David appeared on the scene. By faith, David confronted this giant and made mincemeat of him, enabling the Israeli armies to slaughter the Philistines. Whilst the triumphant army was marching home, the women sang songs of praise, and this happened to be more in favour of David than the reigning king, Saul. The Bible says "from that time, Saul kept a jealous eye on David." He actually hated him to the extent that he tried to kill him on several occasions.

The other examples are the religious leaders in Jesus's time. They were jealous of Jesus and hated him for his popularity. They had been with the people all this while but could not pull the crowd and do the things that Jesus was doing in the few years that he was with them. Eventually their jealousy and hatred led them to kill him:

> The Lord knows people's thoughts; he knows they are worthless. (Psalm 94:11 NLT)

> The Lord detests the thoughts of the wicked, but those of the pure are pleasing to him. (Proverbs 15:26 NIV)

These two scriptures tell us that the Lord knows our thoughts and that he detests all the wicked, hateful, and evil thoughts that we harbour. They are not pleasing to him: "To fear the Lord is to hate evil" (Proverbs 8:13 NIV).

When we reverence the Lord, cherish and love him, we will not entertain hatred in our hearts and end up being bitter. When hateful and evil thoughts occupy your mind all the time, you will not have the peace to think about positive things. Remember what Hesoid wrote: "He harms himself who does evil to another, and the evil plan is most harmful to the planner." Being hateful does not help you in anyway. In the long run, your hatred may turn out to be your Armageddon, a reflection of the case of Haman in the book of Esther.

Hateful and evil thinking will lead you into a lifestyle of murmurings and complaining.

Chapter 5

MURMURING AND COMPLAINING

Murmuring and complaining are twin activities that, when engaged in, do not move anybody forward. You either become stagnant or retrogress. If you want to make progress in life, the best thing to do is to design and implement productive ideas that will bring positive change. If this is true, then I will associate myself with American lawyer and judge Shirley Hufsteddler who said, "You don't make progress by standing on the sidelines, whimpering and complaining. You make progress by implementing ideas."[9] However, there are some people whose business is to complain and criticize whatever they come into contact with and wherever they find themselves. All they can contribute to any given situation is always negative.

To murmur is to make a low and continuous sound, with or without moving the lips, that cannot be described as articulate speech. It is usually a quiet or a private expression of discontent. Murmuring is a condition through which one expresses the inner discontent outwardly without much noise. It is always a rejection of one's situation or something. Continuous murmuring, complaining, whining, and nagging are likely to make a person bitter. If you dig deep into the reasons that people murmur and complain continuously, you will sometimes realize that unforgiveness has a role. Even if it is discontentment about a certain situation, you will notice that, if somebody were to be forgiven for something, the situation would be different. When you don't forgive, it is very easy for you to complain about whatever the other person does or a given situation presents. Miriam and Aaron stood against the leadership of Moses. They complained so much that God had to come in. Some elders of Israel also were against Aaron and Moses, and at a certain point in time, the whole of Israel also came along. It does not matter who you are, even if God were to come down to say that you are special, some people would still complain and murmur about you.

Complaining and murmuring has always been part of human behaviour. Humans have never been satisfied with themselves, what they have, what they are, and sometimes what they perceive they will be.

We complain to show our discontent about other people or situations. Everyone has complained about something at one point in time or another in his or her life. This is not the kind of complaining that makes a person bitter; however, when this complaining becomes a habit or a routine, then it grows into something else.

Let's take a look at this scripture: "I loathe my very life; therefore I will give free rein to my complaint and speak out in the bitterness of my soul" (Job 10:1 NIV).

Job, in his distress, complained, and I am sure if I had been in his shoes, I would have done the same thing. Job was honest to say that he was bitter. His constant complaining concerning his suffering made him so.

Murmuring and complaining are always against somebody, a system or a situation. Let us take a look at some of the people and systems who suffered from the effects of murmuring and complaining in the Bible.

First we'll look at murmuring against Moses:

> They said to Moses, "Was it because there were no graves in Egypt that you brought us to the desert to die? What have you done to us by bringing us out of Egypt? Didn't we say to you in Egypt, 'Leave us alone; let us serve the Egyptians'? It would have been better for us to serve the Egyptians than to die in the desert!" (Exodus 14:11–12 NIV)

> So the people grumbled against Moses, saying, "What are we to drink?" (Exodus 15:24 NIV)

> But the people were thirsty for water there, and they grumbled against Moses. They said, "Why did you bring us up out of Egypt to make us and our children and livestock die of thirst?" (Exodus 17:3 NIV)

It is interesting to note the grumblings and complaints of a people who were once under bondage. So soon they had forgotten how the Lord delivered them through the same Moses. All they were concerned about was the challenges they were facing. They cared less about what had happened. The good past had no meaning for them. This is how murmuring and complaining leads you to sin. You become ungrateful, paranoid, and refuse to see all the good the Lord has done for you. Can you say categorically that you cannot find any blessing of God in your life? Think about it. That is why song writer Johnson Oatman Jr., in his hymn, "Count Your Blessings," wrote: "Count your blessings, name them one by one, count your blessings, see what God has done! Count your blessings, name them one by one, and it will surprise you what the Lord has done." This is very true. The fact that you even have what it takes to count your blessings shows that all is not negative.

> Miriam and Aaron began to talk against Moses because of his Cushite wife, for he had married a Cushite. "Has the Lord spoken only through Moses?" they asked. "Hasn't he also spoken through us?" And the Lord heard this. (Numbers 12:1–2 NIV)

> They came as a group to oppose Moses and Aaron and said to them, "You have gone too far! The whole community is holy, every one of them, and the Lord is with them. Why then do you set yourselves above the Lord's assembly?" (Numbers 16:3 NIV)

> The next day the whole Israelite community grumbled against Moses and Aaron. "You have killed the Lord's people," they said. (Numbers 16:41 NIV)

We notice from the Bible accounts of the exodus from Egypt to the Promised Land that the Israelites on many occasions murmured and complained against Moses, as well as his brother and sister, Aaron and Miriam. They murmured about situations for which they were dissatisfied. And, unfortunately for them, their complaints were not only against Moses; they were also basically against God who had brought them out of Egypt and was taking them to the Promised Land. Whenever they complained and murmured, God solved their problem, but sometimes with an accompanying punishment, which I believe made some people angry and bitter. Does this situation tell us anything? I am inclined to think that, instead of complaining and murmuring, they could have turned their challenges into prayer concerning whatever the complaint was. There have been several times when I have had to remind myself of this. One may also ask why God punished the complainers. I think murmuring and complaining portray God as incapable of handling a situation or solving a problem because, you see, no problem is bigger than God.

> They grumbled in their tents and did not obey the Lord. So he swore to them with uplifted hand that he would make them fall in the desert, make their descendants fall among the nations and scatter them throughout the lands. (Psalm 106 25–27 NIV)

> Now the people complained about their hardships in the hearing of the Lord, and when he heard them his anger was aroused. Then fire from the Lord burned among them and consumed some of the outskirts of the camp. When the people cried out to Moses, he prayed to the Lord and the fire died down. So that place was called Taberah, because fire from the Lord had burned among them. (Numbers 11:1–4 NIV)

In the New Testament we also see some examples of murmuring and complaining against Jesus by the Pharisees and the teachers of the law.

> But the Pharisees and the teachers of the law muttered, "This man welcomes sinners and eats with them." (Luke 15:2 NIV)

> All the people saw this and began to mutter, "He has gone to be the guest of a sinner." (Luke 19:7 NIV)

Murmuring and complaining shows we have no faith in God. It is evidence of doubting the goodness and the capacity of God, and no doubter receives any blessing from him. God is a sovereign God. He is not accountable to anybody. He does what pleases him, and therefore, murmuring against him is a great risk and an exercise in futility. God loves and cares about you. Instead of complaining and murmuring, let him know your problems with thanksgiving, supplication, and intercessions.

> One of you will say to me: "Then why does God still blame us? For who resists his will?" But who are you, O man, to talk back to God? "Shall what is formed say to him who formed it, 'Why did you make me like this?' Does not the potter have the right to make out of the same lump of clay some pottery for noble purposes and some for common use?" (Romans 9:19–21 NIV)

Why do people murmur and complain?

1. Some do it when they are dissatisfied with something when they compare it to the descriptions given to them early on.

Cain was angry with Abel and God, and this turned into hatred and bitterness. Abel's "crime" was the acceptance of his offering, and God's was his refusal to accept Cain's offering. Couldn't Cain have pleaded with God or found out what kind of offering was acceptable to him and later done the right thing? The anger and bitterness emanating from all his complaints did not help him.

2.   Sometimes, people do it in order not to be blamed. Some people resort to complaining about a situation before accusing fingers are pointed at them, and if they are not successful in getting the blame shifted, they become angry and bitter.

3.   Some people murmur and complain when they are treated unfairly, especially when they are unable to confront those who treated them that way. Have you ever been unfairly treated, wrongly accused, or abused? What was your reaction then, and what is it today? The anger and hatred is even greater when it is a trusted close relation who had wronged you.

4.   When they are jealous of someone or some others, some people sometimes resort to complaining about everything these people do or say. There is an adage in Ghana that says that when somebody is envious or jealous of you, even the sight of your dog makes you angry.

5.   When sinners prosper, righteous people tend to complain and murmur, especially when they are not prospering even though they are serving God faithfully.

> You are always righteous, O Lord, when I bring
> a case before you. Yet I would speak with you

about your justice: Why does the way of the wicked prosper? Why do all the faithless live at ease? (Jeremiah 12:1 NIV)

When you toil day and night, pay your tithe, and do all the right things and yet do not see any improvement in the quality of your life, you may begin to question the propriety of your righteousness. But know that the way of the unrighteous is a slippery one.

When injustice or partiality is perpetrated against them, whether at the workplace, in the family, or in society in general, human beings will complain. Some people have found themselves in prison due to wrong identity or accusations. How can you serve this prison term without murmuring and complaining, being angry and bitter when you know clearly in your heart of hearts that you are innocent? However, you have no right to complain when your sins and offences are great.

For I know how many are your offenses and how great your sins. You oppress the righteous and take bribes and you deprive the poor of justice in the courts. (Amos 5:12 NIV)

6. Sometimes people complain when they do not have the full understanding or facts of a situation, and this permeates so many areas of human life. When civil society does not understand government policy and does not know the facts behind the figures as presented, there is bound to be complaining and murmuring, if not demonstrations.

When church members can't see what their financial contributions are being used for, they are likely to murmur and complain. The list of reasons are endless.

Effects of murmuring and complaining

Murmuring and complaining tempts and provokes God to anger:

> So they quarrelled with Moses and said, "Give us water to drink." Moses replied, "Why do you quarrel with me? Why do you put the Lord to the test?" (Exodus 17:2 NIV)

> We should not test the Lord, as some of them did—and were killed by snakes. And do not grumble, as some of them did—and were killed by the destroying angel. (1 Corinthians 10:9–10 NIV)

Complaining and murmuring have never helped anyone. They create a polluted atmosphere and facilitate demonic attacks and unbridled demonic operations. The devil thrives so much in such situations.

> Do everything without complaining or arguing, so that you may become blameless and pure, children of God without fault in a crooked and depraved generation, in which you shine like stars in the universe. (Philippians 2:14–16 NIV)

It is evidently clear that complaining and murmuring do not bring the blessings of God, and even antagonize him. Who wants to antagonize God? Anyone who is not blessed in this state tends to be bitter if the "dry season of blessing" persists for a long while, and this can lead to some sort of mental and spiritual slavery.

Chapter 6

THE FETTERS OF SLAVERY

The issue of slavery is a question of state of mind. If you are not enslaved in your mind, then the likelihood for you to be enslaved in any other way is quite remote. Slavery is such a wicked thing that, over the years, people have fought against it, some even to the extent of losing their lives. If you read some history books on slavery, you will wonder how some human beings were able to do that against humanity.

What is slavery?

Slavery is a state of being completely dominated by another. Slaves are considered personal property and are subjected to involuntary servitude.

Who then is a slave?

- A person who is owned by somebody else
- A person who is forced to work without pay
- A person who is dominated by somebody or by something
- A person who meekly accepts being totally controlled by another person

How can a person be enslaved?

"The moment the slave resolves that he will no longer be a slave, his fetters fall. Freedom and slavery are mental states."[10] I wonder how many people will disagree with Mahatma Gandhi, leader of the Indian independence movement, on this issue. Not even a government or political system can maintain you as a slave if you decide in your mind that enough is enough.

From these definitions, we understand that a slave is someone who is dominated by somebody or something. There are so many things that are dominating people's lives in this 21st century. Some of these are the love of money, sex, drugs, unending acquisition of degrees, lottery, alcohol, friends, jobs or businesses, the quest for power, fits of rage, homosexuality, pornography, mobile phones and other technology, witchcraft, social groups, football clubs, political party activities, and so forth "They promise them freedom, while they themselves are slaves of depravity—for *'people are slaves to whatever has mastered them'*" (2 Peter 2:19 NIV, emphasis mine)

The Bible tells us that a man is a slave to whatever dominates and rules his life. Have you ever come across a drug addict who cannot get his drug when he needs it? He or she, I am told, is a pathetic sight. Until he gets it, he is never free to move on with his life. This is complete bondage or slavery. That is why a drug addict will go to every length to make sure he or she gets what he or she wants, even if it means killing someone. They cannot help but to obey the master's call. "Jesus replied, 'I tell you the truth, everyone who sins is a slave to sin'" (John 8:34 NLT).

Types of slavery:

1. Sin is a slave master, and this master knows only one thing, and that is to get you to hell. This will be explained further when we discuss the effects of bitterness.

   > For when we were controlled by the sinful nature, the sinful passions aroused by the law were at work in our bodies, so that we bore fruit for death. (Romans 7:5 NIV)

   > Don't you know that when you offer yourselves to someone to obey him as slaves, you are slaves to the one whom you obey—whether you are slaves to sin, which leads to death, or to obedience, which leads to righteousness? (Romans 6:16 NIV)

   Everyone who makes a practice of sin is a slave to sin. Sin slavery brings death, whereas slavery to Jesus brings freedom. This is a paradox. The discussion of this will be for another time. The Bible says the wages of sin is death, but the gift of God is eternal life through Christ. Are you a slave to sin? Is there any sin which is dominating your life and making you miserable and bitter? Stop behaving as if all is well with you and confront the source of your bitterness (enslavement to sin). "The evil deeds of a wicked man ensnare him; the cords of his sin hold him fast" (Proverbs 5:22 NIV).

2. Another form of slavery, which is common and accepted by all as slavery, is forced labour with no payment. Additionally, the enforcers consider the slaves as personal property. This is what happened to the people of Israel in Egypt, and the Bible says their lives were made bitter. Who would not be bitter in this situation? As a result of poverty and other issues, some young men and women from Africa are being forced into prostitution in some developed countries, and they earn virtually nothing for their sorrows and labour. Some of these young people are so bitter against society that they will do anything deviant to pay back.

> They made their lives bitter with hard labor in brick and mortar and with all kinds of work in the fields; in all their hard labor the Egyptians used them ruthlessly. (Exodus 1:14 NIV)

> The Lord had seen how bitterly everyone in Israel, whether slave or free, was suffering; there was no one to help them. (2 Kings 14:26 NIV)

The devil has enslaved so many people in all kinds of situations, and has not provided them with any good reward. He is using them to do his dirty work and rewarding them with things that are detrimental to their health and well-being.

There are a lot of young people on the streets of this country who are so bitter with society because of their economic enslavement. The issue is, when will these people be liberated and by whom? The government does not have what it takes to do that; if it had, it wouldn't have taken us over fifty years to get into this mess. It's about time you took your destiny into your own hands legitimately, by seeking the face of God and thinking seriously about what you can do with your life. Stop looking up to the government, and your murmuring and complaining will abate. You will also, by so doing, free yourself from the incompetence and insensitivities of our governments.

3.   One can also be enslaved by sickness or disease as exemplified in Luke 13:10–11. When a person has been sick for a long time without remedy, he or she comes under the dominion of the disease and literally become enslaved. The thinking and behaviour is dominated and dictated by this sickness. Let's face facts here. The tendency to become bitter and disappointed is very great if your faith is not strong or you do not receive encouragement from loved ones. Even if you have a strong faith it can be shaken seriously and this is how sometimes people become bitter against God. You are likely to ask, why me?

> On a Sabbath Jesus was teaching in one of the synagogues, and a woman was there who had been crippled by a spirit for eighteen years. She was bent over and could not straighten up at all. (Luke 13:10–11 NIV)

What are the characteristics of a slave?

It is important to know some of the characteristics of a slave so that, when you begin to see some of these signs in your life, you take action before you are caught in the net and end up being bitter.

A slave has no choice of his or her own. A slave's fate is dictated by the master. A slave is controlled by another person or a situation and is forced to do what he or she may not like. The slave submits to the authority of another person or situation, which is very often detrimental. With these kinds of characteristics, who can tell me that this is not a fertile ground for bitterness? "For I see that you are full of bitterness and captive to sin" (Acts 8:23 NIV).

For the past few years, Ghana has been dominated by two political parties. The rivalry and bitterness between these parties has affected all aspects of national life such that the only thing left without political colour is the air we breathe. I don't know what will happen to this air in the next ten years if the situation does not change. This kind of bitterness has affected the populace so much that many a time we are unable to discuss national issues "sensibly" or dispassionately without any political colouration. As Acts 8:23 expresses, the whole nation has virtually become enslaved or "bewitched" by these two political parties, and their sin of bitterness is dividing the nation against itself. As I stated in my introduction, "Bitterness is a condition lived in a bitter atmosphere, infested with acrimony or hatred, sealed and polished with pretence. In this pretentious atmosphere silence shouts louder than words." The day this silence will take on a "voice" expressing the bitterness pent up inside, it might not augur well for us as a people. The sooner we get rid of all these bitter yokes put on our necks by these political parties and call them to order, the better it will be for us all as Ghanaians.

> As obedient children, do not conform to the evil
> desires you had when you lived in ignorance.
> But just as he who called you is holy, so be holy
> in all you do; for it is written: "Be holy, because
> I am holy." (1 Peter 1:14–16 NIV)

As a child of God, nothing should enslave you except the love of Christ. Yielding yourself to the evil desires of this world will make you a slave of this world of sin and set you up in bitter contention with your God. You deserve better than that.

Chapter 7

THE PROUD HEART

Pride will always keep you in trouble either with God or with men. It is a cover up for our faults, an admission of our weakness and in fact ready to bring you down at any moment. Someone once said, "Temper gets you into trouble. Pride keeps you there."[11] It will keep you there because of the fear of change. This kind of fear is an admission of weakness as demonstrated by American Catholic Archbishop Fulton J. Sheen in this quote: "Pride is an admission of weakness; it secretly fears all competition and dreads all rivals."[12]

What is pride?

Pride is born from an excessively high opinion of oneself. It inspires arrogance and a disdainful, haughty, conceited disposition. In a negative sense, it is a preoccupation with one's self, inspiring self-exaltation, a feeling of superiority, and behaviour that arrogantly steps on others and has an independent spirit that rules out the rule of God. This is conceited superiority. It is all about the "me" factor.

The "sin of pride" is considered by some people as the greatest sin or the root of all sins. The sin of pride turned Lucifer into Satan, the devil. When you give credit to yourself for what God has done, you prove to be proud.

Where then does pride come from?

Pride originates from the heart; it is an emotional state that one chooses to be in. It is an evil that comes from within to defile you. This is one of the reasons that you ought to guard your heart.

> For from within, out of the heart of men, proceed evil thoughts, adulteries, fornications, murders, thefts, covetousness, wickedness, deceit, lasciviousness, an evil eye, blasphemy, pride, foolishness: all these evil things come from within, and defile the man. (Mark 7:21– 23 KJV)

The Bible says that all the issues of life emanates from the heart; therefore, it is not surprising why pride originates from the heart. Every kind of defilement separates you from God, and since pride is a defilement, it will certainly separate you from him. This situation is too expensive to be entertained. Who can afford to be separated from his maker? The moment you are separated from God, know that sin has come in. This is why you have to guard your heart seriously.

Pride is sin as stated in Proverbs 21:4: "Haughty eyes and a proud heart, and evil actions are all sin!" (NLT). And, "Guard your heart above all else, for it determines the course of your life" (Proverbs 4:23 NLT)

Why is pride mentioned first when God talks of the things he hates most? I believe pride is the root of many sins and   a serious abomination to the Lord. He hates it. All of the following scriptures go to show that God is really opposed to and hates pride or the proud.

> These six things doth the Lord hate: yea, seven are an abomination unto him: A proud look, a lying tongue, and hands that shed innocent blood. (Proverbs 6:16–18 KJV)

> Every one that is proud in heart is an abomination to the Lord: though hand join in hand, he shall not be unpunished. (Proverbs 16:5 KJV)

> The fear of the Lord is to hate evil: pride, and arrogancy, and the evil way, and the forward mouth, do I hate. (Proverbs 8:13 KJV)

Characteristics and facts about proud people

What are some of the characteristics o a proud person? We need to understand some of the characteristics or facts about a proud person and this will help us to see why pride can lead to bitterness. Here are six characteristics or facts about a proud person:

1. **Proud people are arrogant.** Arrogance is an attitude of superiority or self-importance or over bearing pride, all of which are offensive. This is the foremost reason why I believe God hates pride. Arrogance is an affront to God. It shows no respect to him and places the proud person first in everything. The arrogant person is a God mocker as indicated in this scripture: "The proud and arrogant

man—'Mocker' is his name; he behaves with overwhelming pride" (Proverbs 21:24 NIV).

2. **Proud people indulge in self-importance and self-justification.** If you are too important and justified in your own eyes, then you don't need God, as exemplified in the following story:

> Two men went to the Temple to pray. One was a Pharisee, and the other was a despised tax collector. The Pharisee stood by himself and prayed this prayer: "I thank you, God, that I am not a sinner like everyone else. For I don't cheat, I don't sin, and I don't commit adultery. I'm certainly not like that tax collector! I fast twice a week, and I give you a tenth of my income."
>
> But the tax collector stood at a distance and dared not even lift his eyes to heaven as he prayed. Instead, he beat his chest in sorrow, saying, "O God, be merciful to me, for I am a sinner." I tell you, this sinner, not the Pharisee, returned home justified before God. For those who exalt themselves will be humbled, and those who humble themselves will be exalted. (Luke 18:10–14 NLT)

The person who is important in his or her own eyes exalts him or herself, but the Lord will bring such a person down.

3. **Proud people hate God, and have no confidence in him.** The proud person has confidence only in him or herself and never thinks about God for anything. Whatever the equation is, everything is by the proud person's ability and

skills: "In his pride the wicked does not seek him; in all his thoughts there is no room for God" (Psalm 10:4).

4. **Proud people practice self-deception.** This is a major component of the characteristics of the proud. Deceiving yourself about what you are not leads to your downfall. The proud person, most of the time, misses the opportunity to be real, and how long can one remain unreal?

"Most of our platitudes notwithstanding, self-deception remains the most difficult deception. The tricks that work on others count for nothing in that very well-lit back alley where one keeps assignations with oneself: no winning smiles will do here, no prettily drawn lists of good intentions."[13] Self-deception, according to American author Joan Didio is the most difficult deception to deal with. Until the person is able to recognize and accept reality as defined and stated in scripture (if the person is a Christian) concerning anything, it is virtually impossible to deal with this deception.

> "The terror you inspire and the pride of your
> heart have deceived you, you who live in the
> clefts of the rocks, who occupy the heights of
> the hill. Though you build your nest as high as
> the eagle's, from there I will bring you down,"
> declares the Lord. (Jeremiah 49:16 NIV)

For example, a person can be deceived that because of his or her connections with the powers that be in a society he or she is an untouchable, but the scripture above tells me that the person is just ready to be brought down heavily and disgraced. This assertion is emphasized by the scripture in Obadiah:

"The pride of your heart has deceived you, you who live in the clefts of the rocks and make your home on the heights, you who say to yourself, 'Who can bring me down to the ground?' Though you soar like the eagle and make your nest among the stars, from there I will bring you down," declares the Lord. (Obadiah 1:3–4 NIV)

5. **Proud people prosecute others.** And they prosecute just because it is within their power to do so. This is sometimes done to show the weak "where power lies." "In his arrogance the wicked man hunts down the weak, who are caught in the schemes he devises" (Psalm 10:2 NIV).

6. **Proud people are self-righteousness.** This leads to the denial of God, and there is the need for repentance and forgiveness. This is the last straw that kills the proud. Where there is no repentance, there is no forgiveness, and where there is no forgiveness, there is no remission of sins.

To some who were confident of their own righteousness and looked down on everybody else, Jesus told this parable: "Two men went up to the temple to pray, one a Pharisee and the other a tax collector. The Pharisee stood up and prayed about himself: 'God, I thank you that I am not like other men—robbers, evildoers, adulterers—or even like this tax collector. I fast twice a week and give a tenth of all I get.' But the tax collector stood at a distance. He would not even look up to heaven, but beat his breast and said, 'God, have mercy on me, a sinner.'" (Luke 18:9–13 NIV)

How does pride affect a person? There is no positive effect of negative pride.

Eight direct effects of pride on a person's life.

1. God resists the proud. Your whole life depends on grace, even the air you breathe. If God decides to withdraw that grace, where will you be? If he decides to oppose you, where will your locus be? But he gives us more grace. That is why Scripture says: "Go opposes the proud but gives grace to the humble" (James 4:6 NIV).

2. God subdues and humiliates the proud. Haman is a classic example of a proud person who was subdued and humiliated by God. He thought he had all the power and the right to annihilate the Jews in Babylon. He boasted of his connections to the top, but God was not pleased with that. His arrogance ended him on the gallows he built for others (Esther 7).

    > Now I know that the Lord is greater than all other gods, for he did this to those who had treated Israel arrogantly. (Exodus 18:11 NIV)

    > I will punish the world for its evil, the wicked for their sins. I will put an end to the arrogance of the haughty and will humble the pride of the ruthless. (Isaiah 13:11 NIV)

    The proud are brought into contempt and humbled. For example, when some people become rich, they tend to be proud, and this has landed some in conditions of nothingness in no time. Sometimes when some people are elevated or promoted at the workplace or in any endeavour, pride sets in, and they begin to look down on those under them: "The Lord Almighty planned it, to bring low the pride of all glory and to humble all who are renowned on the earth" (Isaiah 23:9 NIV).

3.	The proud are also brought low and abased. There is a day coming when the proud will be humbled. You may think everything is under your proud control now, but know that there is a day in store for the humiliation (bringing low) of the proud.

> You save the humble but bring low those whose eyes are haughty. (Psalm 18:27 NIV)

> The Lord Almighty has a day in store for all the proud and lofty, for all that is exalted (and they will be humbled). (Isaiah 2:12 NIV)

> Now I, Nebuchadnezzar, praise and exalt and glorify the King of heaven, because everything he does is right and all his ways are just. And those who walk in pride he is able to humble. (Daniel 4:37 NIV)

> For whoever exalts himself will be humbled, and whoever humbles himself will be exalted. (Matthew 23:12 NIV)

The proud are paid back in full according to the level of evil committed in relation to their pride or arrogance. Here again, Haman is a good example as shown in Esther chapter 7. Also, "Love the Lord, all his saints! The Lord preserves the faithful, but the proud he pays back in full" (Psalm 31:23 NIV).

4.   Destruction is followed by shame.

"Temper gets you into trouble. Pride keeps you there" (Unknown).

This is too obvious, and is substantiated by these scriptures:

When pride comes, then comes disgrace, but with humility comes wisdom. (Proverbs 11:2 NIV)

A man's pride brings him low, but a man of lowly spirit gains honor. (Proverbs 29:23 NIV)

That wreath, the pride of Ephraim's drunkards, will be trampled underfoot. (Isaiah 28:3 NIV)

Pride goes before destruction, a haughty spirit before a fall. (Proverbs 16:18 NIV)

Before his downfall a man's heart is proud, but humility comes before honor. (Proverbs 18:12 NIV)

5.   Pride encourages a contentious spirit. The proud person develops a contentious spirit and stirs up strife. Absalom was contentious and stirred up strife, which ended in the death of Amnon. His pride led him to stage a coup d'état against his father, which eventually caused his death.

Pride only breeds quarrels, but wisdom is found in those who take advice. (Proverbs 13:10 NIV)

He that is of a proud heart stirreth up strife: but he that putteth his trust in the Lord shall be made fat. (Proverbs 28:25 KJV)

6.   Pride is likely to lead other people to reject the word of God. Every human being knows some people who agree or see eye to eye with him or her on some issues. Even wicked and devilish political dictators have supporters. Murderers sometimes have accomplices. This therefore implies that, when this proud person is becoming lost, it is likely he or she will take others with him or her.

> Azariah son of Hoshaiah and Johanan son of Kareah and all the other proud men said to Jeremiah, "You lie! The Lord our God hasn't forbidden us to go to Egypt! Baruch son of Neriah has convinced you to say this, because he wants us to stay here and be killed by the Babylonians or be carried off into exile." So Johanan and the other guerrilla leaders and all the people refused to obey the Lord's command to stay in Judah. Johanan and the other leaders took with them all the people who had returned from the nearby countries to which they had fled. In the crowd were men, women, and children, the king's daughters, and all those whom Nebuzaradan, the captain of the guard, had left with Gedaliah. The prophet Jeremiah and Baruch were also included. The people refused to obey the voice of the Lord and went to Egypt, going as far as the city of Tahpanhes. (Jeremiah 43:2–7 NIV)

This story shows how some arrogant men, in their pride, rejected the word of God and led other people to disobey God. The proud always think they know better, and in their overconfidence, they persuade or force others to follow them.

How then does pride make a person bitter?

Looking at all the effects of pride on a person, is it any wonder that a proud person could be a bitter person? When God resists a proud person like Nebuchadnezzar, brings him into contempt, subdues and brings him low, brings him to shame, rejects and pays him back in full for all his sins, the logical result is anger and bitterness in the long run. It takes grace for a proud person to acknowledge his pride and seek help or do something about it himself or herself. Are you wondering why you are where you are today after enjoying a certain level of a good life some time back? May I humbly suggest you check your "pride level"? How do you do that? Look at the life of the Lord Jesus Christ and learn from him. He is our best example. Pride will always lead you to a life of self-justification, an evil in the sight of God.

Chapter 8

THE SELF-JUSTIFICATION HAZARD

A treacherous servant will betray you when you need him most. That is why I agree with former New York Giants' co-owner Wellington Mara when he say, "Self-justification is a treacherous servant."[14] A treacherous servant will betray your trust and faith and prove himself or herself to be a disloyal person. In the same vein, self-justification will sustain or keep you in good stead just for a period. It is not sustainable; it has an expiry date.

What is self-justification?

Self-justification is making excuses and explanations for oneself or one's behaviour. It is done to prove oneself or one's actions right and reasonable.

So how do people try to justify themselves?

Four ways by which people justify themselves.

1. **Not accepting their wrongdoing.** Instead, people make excuses for daily failures and justifying their position.

    Typical examples of self-justification can be seen in the stories of Adam and Eve, Cain and Abel.

    > He answered, "I heard you in the garden, and I was afraid because I was naked; so I hid." And he said, "Who told you that you were naked? Have you eaten from the tree that I commanded you not to eat from?" The man said, "The woman you put here with me—she gave me some fruit from the tree, and I ate it." Then the Lord God said to the woman "What is this you have done?" The woman said "The serpent deceived me, and I ate." (Genesis 3:10– 13 NIV)

    > Then the Lord said to Cain, "Where is your brother Abel?" "I don't know," he replied. "Am I my brother's keeper?" (Genesis 4:9 NIV)

    In these two scriptures, you will realize that, when the sins of the people involved were discovered, their first reactions were to justify themselves. Adam justified himself by putting the blame on God whilst Cain rejected any responsibility towards his brother. It is not always very easy for any human being to admit that he or she was wrong in any given situation. The tendency is to make excuses as stated in the definitions given here. The attempt at justifying yourself very often leads to lies in succession, and sometimes leads to offence against others.

The following scriptures shows that God does not approve of our attempts to justify ourselves when we sin, when we are unproductive, or when we undertake our responsibilities with careless abandon and try to find excuses to justify our carelessness. When we are unable to fulfil our vows, pay our tithes and offerings, or fulfil promises we make to people, God is also not pleased.

> But there was a certain man named Ananias who, with his wife, Sapphira, sold some property. He brought part of the money to the apostles, claiming it was the full amount. With his wife's consent, he kept the rest.

> Then Peter said, "Ananias, why have you let Satan fill your heart? You lied to the Holy Spirit, and you kept some of the money for yourself. The property was yours to sell or not sell, as you wished. And after selling it, the money was also yours to give away. How could you do a thing like this? You weren't lying to us but to God!"

> As soon as Ananias h ard these words, he fell to the floor and died. Everyone who heard about it was terrified. Then some young men got up, wrapped him in a sheet, and took him out and buried him.

> About three hours later his wife came in, not knowing what had happened. Peter asked her, "Was this the price you and your husband received for your land?"

> "Yes," she replied, "that was the price."

And Peter said, "How could the two of you even think of conspiring to test the Spirit of the Lord like this? The young men who buried your husband are just outside the door, and they will carry you out, too."

Instantly, she fell to the floor and died. When the young men came in and saw that she was dead, they carried her out and buried her beside her husband. Great fear gripped the entire church and everyone else who heard what had happened. (Acts 5:1–11 NLT)

Ananias and his wife Sapphira sought to justify themselves for what they did, but God was not impressed, and this cost them their lives. Self-justification, which never admits wrong-doing, is always likely to end up in disaster, which is a recipe for anger, hatred, and bitterness.

"The sluggard says, 'There is a lion outside!' or, 'I will be murdered in the streets!'" (Proverbs 22:13 NIV) This is the self- justification of the lazy person. There is always an excuse for why he or she cannot work or do something. What will be the result? Poverty, of course. And when others are prospering, they become angry and sometimes go to the extent of maligning or accusing the prosperous one of wrongdoing. They become bitter when nobody seems to be agreeing with them or seeing their point of view.

Do not let your mouth lead you into sin. And do not protest to the [temple] messenger, "My vow was a mistake." Why should God be angry at what you say and destroy the work of your hands? (Ecclesiastes 5:6 NIV)

But the third servant brought back only the original amount of money and said, "Master,

I hid your money and kept it safe. I was afraid because you are a hard man to deal with, taking what isn't yours and harvesting crops you didn't plant."

"You wicked servant!" the king roared. "Your own words condemn you. If you knew that I'm a hard man who takes what isn't mine and harvests crops I didn't plant, why didn't you deposit my money in the bank? At least I could have gotten some interest on it."

Then, turning to the others standing nearby, the king ordered, "Take the money from this servant, and give it to the one who has ten pounds."

"But master," they said, "he already has ten pounds!"

"Yes," the kin replied, "and to those who use well what they are given, even more will be given. But from those who do nothing, even what little they have will be taken away." (Luke 19:20–26 NLT)

Here was a servant who was trying hard to justify himself for the actions he had taken, and what he had said about his master. He ended up losing the little he had, and to make matters worse for him, he lost it to another man who had more than he. I can imagine how angry this man would be for losing his job. What would happen if his joblessness prevailed for a long time? The tendency to become bitter would be very high. When you cannot pay your utility bills and children's school fees, and you have to go borrowing before you can feed your family, becoming bitter with yourself or the one who made you jobless is a likely possibility.

Looking at the situation of this servant, we see that he could have given the excuse that working with just one mina was a difficult or an impossible task. He may have been thinking that the master did not like him, life was not fair, and therefore it was not his fault for not being able to use that money. All the excuses he could put together could not help him.

No one can justify him or herself before God. All our good works are like filthy rags before him.

2. **Nobody is perfect.** Sometimes people justify themselves by imputing their mistakes or shortcomings to the fact that they are ordinary human beings (mortals) just like any other fallible person and not superhuman. To them nobody is perfect. Why accuse me alone?

    > All a man's ways seem innocent to him, but motives are weighed by the Lord. (Proverbs 16:2 NIV)

    > All a man's ways seem right to him, but the Lord weighs the heart. (Proverbs 21:2 NIV)

    > You may justify yourself with your human frailty, but God looks at your heart and your motives, which you cannot run away from.

3. **Reaction to criticism.** Criticism is a judgment by a person that points out what is wrong or bad about another person or a situation. How then should one react to criticism?

Every judgment is a measurement against a standard. This could be a national or cultural standard or God's standard. Every negative reaction to criticism puts a person on the path of self-justification. Failure to acknowledge one's faults does not profit anyone.

> Now all has been heard; here is the conclusion of the matter: Fear God and keep his commandments, for this is the whole [duty] of man. For God will bring every deed into judgment, including every hidden thing, whether it is good or evil. (Ecclesiastes 12:13– 14 NIV)

> There will be no forgiveness if there is no confession and repentance. When you cannot come before God because of self-justification, you set yourself on a collision course with him. Who can collide with God and remain the same? You either plead for mercy or become bitter as a result of the consequences of the collision. You will have no legs to stand on afterwards. The only way you can be justified is by faith through the blood of Jesus Christ.

4. **So far as they don't engage in certain vices, they are all right.** If we say we have no sin, then the Bible says we are liars. Some people find it difficult to accept the fact that they are sinners; they justify themselves in that they do not engage in some of the evil things they see other people do. So far as they don't drink, smoke, or go after men or women they are all right, but this scripture tells us that it is not true: "If we claim to be without sin, we deceive ourselves and the truth is not in us" (1 John 1:8–9 NIV) Nobody can claim that he or she is without sin, and we can

also add that the fact that even ef everybody is doing some-thing, that does not make it right, whatever it is.

It is the truth that will set you free. When self-justification fails, the result is anger, frustration, and bitterness. All our good works, the Bible says, are like filthy rags before God; therefore, there is no way you can justify yourself before him. He is the one who justifies us.

Chapter 9

THE POVERTY MENACE

I cannot help but agree with Mother Teresa: "We think sometimes that poverty is only being hungry, naked and homeless.
The poverty of being unwanted, unloved and uncared for is
the greatest poverty. We must start in our own homes to remedy this kind of poverty."[15] Poor people do not have friends
who care, and most of the time, they are lonely. The poor do
not have enough resources to pay for the basic needs of life:
food, clothing, and housing. The poor person who is not content with whatever description of poverty that is placed on him
or her is likely to be angry and bitter, jealous, and sometimes
unappreciative of good things. Poverty is not a good thing. Is
it a choice? Whether it is self-imposed or forced by others or
circumstances, poverty does not make a person happy, and an
unhappy person is most likely an angry and a bitter person as
well.

What are some of the causes of poverty?

There are a myriad of causes, but I will discuss just a few of them here.

1. **Laziness**

> How long will you lie there, you sluggard? When will you get up from your sleep? A little sleep, a little slumber, a little folding of the hands to rest—and poverty will come on you like a bandit and scarcity like an armed man. (Proverbs 6:9–11 NIV)

> Do not love sleep or you will grow poor; stay awake and you will have food to spare. (Proverbs 20:13 NIV)

> A little sleep, a little slumber, a little folding of the hands to rest—and poverty will come on you like a bandit and scarcity like an armed man. (Proverbs 24:33–34 NIV)

> He who works his land will have abundant food, but the one who chases fantasies will have his fill of poverty. (Proverbs 28:19 NIV)

This is one of the major causes of poverty the world over. Inactivity, not seeking to work, and idling about will always result in poverty. Can you imagine graduates forming an association of "unemployed graduates" whiles there are several of our classrooms waiting for teachers? Some of these people are dreaming of working in big organizations and earning fat salaries in an economy like ours. This is chasing fantasies at the moment; however, things may change someday. Why would these people not be poor and bitter? "The wealth of the rich is their fortified city, but poverty is the ruin of the poor" (Proverbs 10:15 NIV).

2. Drunkenness

> Do not join those who drink too much wine or gorge themselves on meat, for drunkards and gluttons become poor, and drowsiness clothes them in rags. (Proverbs 23:20–21 NIV)

If you are sold to alcohol, how can you work or have meaningful relationships that are vital for wealth creation and success? Networking is a very important element in building a clientele base. The success of any business depends on its customers. How can a drunkard maintain customers? What family member would put his resources into the business of a drunkard?

3. Ignoring discipline

> He who ignores discipline comes to poverty and shame. (Proverb 13:18 NIV)

People who ignore discipline or correction in any area of their lives tend to lose in whatever they are doing. For example, ignoring advice from your financial adviser when you are headed for financial disaster will definitely land you in bankruptcy. A farmer who ignores the strict planting discipline required for a particular crop, advised by the extension officer, will definitely have a small harvest at the end of the season. And ignoring the discipline of God the Father will land you squarely in the hands of the devil who, being a devourer, will surely do justice to his description.

4. **Poor treatment by society**

> A poor man is shunned by all his relatives—
> how much more do his friends avoid him!
> Though he pursues them with pleading, they
> are nowhere to be found. (Proverbs 19:7 NIV)

Society sometimes pays lip service to the needs of the poor without concrete action to remedy the situation.

5. **Exploited for personal gains**

> You trample on the poor and force him to give
> you grain. Therefore, though you have built
> stone mansions, you will not live in them;
> though you have planted lush vineyards, you
> will not drink their wine. (Amos 5:11 NIV)

> But you have insulted the poor. Is it not the rich
> who are exploiting you? Are they not the ones
> who are dragging you into court? Are they not
> the ones who are slandering the noble name of
> him to whom you belong? (James 2:6–7 NIV)

People are sometimes made poor by the exploitation of the powerful and the rich in society. Let me illustrate this point with a real-life story. Kwesi sent his car to a mechanic's workshop one Saturday and met a driver whose friends were teasing him that he was a fool for driving a certain gold merchant for three years without salary but only for small, occasional tips. I know some people in developed countries will not understand this issue, but surely some fellow Africans will identify with it. The gold dealer did not know how to drive, and so one day the driver decided to teach him a "little lesson." According to Kwesi, the driver drove the dealer on a business trip from Accra, the capital of Ghana, to a destination that was about two hours away. There he abandoned him on the highway and went back to town. He was fed up with the exploitation. From his conversation and demeanour, everyone could see that he was a bitter person.

6. **Environment**

> When you are born into a family that is poor, and live and grow up in that poor environment, you are likely to continue to be poor if there is no intervention at any point in time. You may never know success and happiness in life just because of your environment. Such a condition can trigger bitterness in a person's life.
>
> English writer William Somerset Maugham stated, "Failure makes people cruel and bitter."[16] Yes, failure can make a person bitter, if the situation of failure persists for a long time but does it really make one cruel?

What are some of the effects of poverty?

1. **Poverty can make a person bitter.** This bitterness can be aimed against God, society, and any individual who is perceived to have played any role in making a person poor.

2. **It's an obstacle to future success.** Obviously, when a person is poor, he or she is disadvantaged in so many ways. For example, the person may not be able to get the best education, nutrition, medical care, and other societal ben-

efits; however, it does not mean that is the end for the person. There is still hope so far as you have life and God.

3. **Poverty can cause people to have a low self-esteem.** There is the tendency for the person to look down on himself or herself as compared to others. An inferiority complex can set in.

4. **The likelihood of engaging in unlawful acts is great.** If the fear of God does not come in, poverty can lead to high levels of stress that, in turn, lead to crime and bitterness against society. Unemployment thus can lead to crime due to depression and need.

5. **Poverty can encourage a negative outlook of one's self when the poverty is generat onal and has become a family culture.** Generat on a ter generation, the situation is the same. Why would a person not think that the family is cursed or that God does not care about them? Would the person be wrong in thinking that there is a witch somewhere responsible for that situation, especially in our part of the world where superstition is very strong? You have the power to break whatever is the cause of this situation if you will depend on Jehovah.

In Ghana where poverty affects the greater part of the population, you can always feel the frustration and anger of the people. Sometimes when you listen to people who phone in to a radio programme to express an opinion, you can literally feel their anger and frustration, especially when the subject of the programme is politicians who don't seem to understand the suffering of the poor. Looking at the effects of poverty on a person, especially when the person has come to the point of low self-esteem, we see there is a high probability of the person becoming bitter against society and some individuals. Some rich people with their opulence and arrogance also aggravate or exacerbate the "bitterness level" of the downtrodden.

Chapter 10

FRUSTRATION

In writing this book, I encountered times when I felt frustrated in a way, in that sometimes my mind "froze" and there were no ideas or words to write. Sometimes I asked myself, "Who is forcing you to write? Is it compulsory that you should be an author?" These questions created a sort of internal conflict because I knew well that my writing is God inspired. You must note here that the fact that God asked you to do something does not mean there will be no problems. You will be frustrated one way or another, especially when the devil knows that, if you succeed in what you are doing, his kingdom will be worse off. Therefore, know that, if God asked you to do it, then he is capable of finishing it with you—like this book you have in your hand.

American author Elizabeth Drew once said, "The torment of human frustration, whatever its immediate cause, is the knowledge that the self is in prison, its vital force and 'mangled mind' leaking away in lonely, wasteful self-conflict."[17] She is right in the sense that, when you feel imprisoned in any way, or incapable of dealing effectively with a situation, the tendency to become frustrated is great. Your situation could be worse if you tried to find solace in people. American football player and coach Lou Holtz will tell you, "Don't tell your problems to people: eighty percent don't care; and the other twenty percent are glad you have them."[18] Not many people care about your problems, but even if they do, most of them may not be in a position to help you in any way. Yes, some may even be happy that you have those problems. Imagine finding out that a close friend is rejoicing over your challenges. It could be very frustrating, and also it could make you angry if not bitter against that person.

What is frustration?

Frustration is the emotion of annoyance that comes from not being able to attain our goals. It can also come from being hindered or criticized.

A frustrated person is an angry person, not a happy person. A frustrated person is often, at the same time, irritable. Frustration also brings on disappointment over being prevented from attaining or reaching certain goals at a certain point in time. Plans may have been torn apart due to somebody's actions or inactions, but nobody seems to care. There is a choice you have to make when your plans are frustrated, hindered, or criticized in a negative way. You either stay frustrated or try to understand the source of the frustration and deal with it accordingly. This may sound ridiculous, but that is exactly what Jesus did when he was being crucified. He sympathized with his killers and asked the Father to forgive them because they did not know what they were doing. They thought they were helping God. They thought they were serving the purpose of God, but they were completely wrong. You can choose to be angry or forgiving, compassionate or inconsiderate, insisting on your right or letting go. Continuous frustration is a sure recipe for a build-up to bitterness.

Taking into consideration the meanings of frustration, you will notice that it is either a result of what one cannot get, or some impediment that has been put in one's way, preventing the achievement of some goals. There is always the likelihood that someone will thwart your plans one way or another. Everything will not always go your way, and that is life. Sometimes you have to accept life like that. I am not saying you should accept anything that comes your way; rather, you should know that there will be certain things you cannot change. Just leave them to God. How long can you be frustrated for the loss of a loved one, for example? How long can you be angry with God for taking that person away? This attitude has to change at some point because it is unsustainable and unhelpful.

What are some of the cause of frustration?

Frustration is an emotional behaviour in response to difficult unresolved problems or opposition. There are so many reasons for frustration. These may include economic, family, business, academic, employment, or spiritual issues among others. In my part of our world, there are many people whose dreams have been frustrated or truncated as a result of parents not being able to pay their school fees or cater for their upkeep. This represents broken promises. Some parents are facing the wrath of their frustrated children just because they have been too busy to pay any attention to them. Some of these offspring are very bitter against their parents and will not have anything to do with them. This situation usually occurs when these individuals are generally unable to make ends meet or lead a very fruitful life. A lot of fathers are facing the wrath and frustrations of their grown-up children because of their refusal or inability to live up to their responsibilities as fathers. I was not surprised at all that during the celebration of one Father's Day, all our airwaves were choked with criticisms of fathers. There was little praise. You could hear in the voices of these people that they were really bitter against their fathers because they thought their fathers could have done better for them.

Unfulfilled personal goals and dreams and deficiencies such as lack of confidence and a feeling of inability to deal with or change a situation, frustration with jobs, academic work, non-cooperation of fellow workers, waste of time and energy, and so forth lead to frustration with life. People are also frustrated with their negative emotions, misunderstandings, disappointments, and suspicions. Frustration with parenting because of stubborn children cannot be left out. Not receiving an expected promotion even though qualifications have been met can be frustrating. All these frustrations could be a result of an internal or an outside force at work.

> My days have passed, my plans are shattered, and so are the desires of my heart. (Job 17:11 NIV)

> What strength do I have, that I should still hope? What prospects, that I should be patient? (Job 6:11 NIV)

Who can be more frustrated than a person who has lost hope in life? Job was not only frustrated, he became bitter as a result of his frustration. Frustration takes away your joy and makes you waste away in insecurity and pain in the heart. It could also lead to your downfall or cause you to miss the purpose of God for your life.

> God is indeed good to Israel, to those who have pure hearts. But I had nearly lost confidence; my

faith was almost gone because I was jealous of the proud when I saw that things go well for the wicked. They do not suffer pain; they are strong and healthy. They do not suffer as other people do; they do not have the troubles that others have. And so they wear pride like a necklace and violence like a robe; their hearts pour out evil, and their minds are busy with wicked schemes. They laugh at other people and speak of evil things; they are proud and make plans to oppress others.

They speak evil of God in heaven and give arrogant orders to everyone on earth, so that even God's people turn to them and eagerly believe whatever they say. They say, "God will not know; the Most High will not find out." That is what the wicked are like. They have plenty and are always getting more. Is it for nothing, then, that I have kept myself pure and have not committed sin? O God, you have made me suffer all day long; every morning you have punished me. If I had said such things, I would not be acting as one of your people. I tried to think this problem through, but it was too difficult for me until I went into your Temple. Then I understood what will happen to the wicked.

You will put them in slippery places and make them fall to destruction! They are instantly destroyed; they go down to a horrible end. They are like a dream that goes away in the morning; when you rouse yourself, O Lord, they disappear. When my thoughts were bitter and my feelings were hurt, I was as stupid as an animal; I did not understand you. (Psalm 73:1–6 GNT)

The psalmist's frustration about the seeming prosperity of the proud made him feel hurt and bitter. Just like the psalmist, we sometimes become bitter and frustrated when we are confronted with situations we don't understand.

How can we deal with frustration?

- Accept your actual position, not dreams. Realize your limitations and be realistic. Whatever happens to you in life, accept that it is a reality. Don't run away from the reality. Note that this does not rule out faith, which will say that, in spite of the circumstances, I still believe the word of God.
- Ask if there is anything good. If there is, focus on it.
- Decide what is necessary and eliminate anything that does not add value.
- Think and figure out different solutions or options.
- Start now. Do not indulge in procrastination.
- Have realistic expectations.
- How important is that which is frustrating you? If it is not that important, let it go.

This is what self-help author and coach Chuck Gallozzi has to say concerning how to get rid of frustration: "Would you like to rid yourself of frustration forever? You can if you have a big dream. Mother Teresa's dream was so great it dwarfed the frustration normally associated with poverty, sickness, homelessness, suffering and death. Isn't it interesting to look at things differently and reflect on our own behaviour? If you disagree, I'll try not to be frustrated."[19] What about you?

Chapter 11

RIDICULE, REJECTION, AND DETERIORATION

Ridicule

Ridicule is a deliberate belittling, often with malicious intent. It usually consists of words and actions intended to rouse contempt toward a person or thing.

American writer Dorothy Parker wrote, "I know that there are things that never have been funny, and never will be. And I know that ridicule may be a shield, but it is not a weapon."[20] Ridicule is never funny. It always hurts, and from Dorothy Parker's point of view, you will realize that it may be a shield for the offender to prevent the other from attacking. However, I also think that it could be used as a weapon against opponents. Looking at the definitions of the word, I see that, when ridicule is employed, it deliberately belittles the target and somehow incapacitates the person. It may also kill the self-esteem of those who are offended, sometimes to the extent that they reject themselves. "First of all, you must understand that in the last days scoffers will come, scoffing and following their own evil desires" (2 Peter 3:3 NIV).

Ridiculing is part and parcel of this life, and scriptures even say there will be scoffers who will be at their best against the kingdom of God in the last days. If the kingdom of God can suffer ridicule then, what about us mortal men? You need to brace up for things like this.

WHAT ARE SOME OF THE SOURCES OF RIDICULE?

• Ridicule by friends

> I have become a laughingstock to my friends, though I called upon God and he answered—a mere laughingstock, though righteous and blameless! Men at ease have contempt for misfortune as the fate of those whose feet are slipping. The tents of marauders are undisturbed, and those who provoke God are secure—those who carry their god in their hands. (Job 12:4–6 NIV)

> This is one area where ridicule often takes place. Friends may ridicule you for various reasons for which one could be angry and bitter. When a friend or a familiar person ridicules you for a difficult situation in which you find yourself then you may wonder where else you could turn. Job's friends made him a laughing stock because of his predicament which none of them understood. That is why at one point, Job talked about the bitterness of his soul. (Job 7:11, 10:1)

> Because of all my enemies, I am the utter contempt of my neighbors; I am a dread to my friends—those who see me on the street flee from me. (Psalm 31:11 NIV)

- Ignorant and unbelieving people

Some people dared to ridicule Jesus the Son of God because of ignorance and unbelief.

> When Jesus entered the ruler's house and saw the flute players and the noisy crowd, he said, "Go away. The girl is not dead but asleep." But they laughed at him. (Matthew 9:23–24 NIV)

> He went in and said to them, "Why all this commotion and wailing? The child is not dead but asleep." But they laughed at him. (Mark 5:39–40 NIV)

> Hearing this, Jesus said to Jairus, "Don't be afraid; just believe, and she will be healed." When he arrived at the house of Jairus, he did not let anyone go in with him except Peter, John and James, and the child's father and mother. Meanwhile, all the people were wailing and mourning for her. "Stop wailing," Jesus said. "She is not dead but asleep." They laughed at him, knowing that she was dead. (Luke 8:50–53 NIV)

All these scriptures give credence to the fact that sometimes people ridicule what they don't know or understand. Even at the crucifixion of Jesus he was ridiculed because the people were spiritually ignorant of what was taking place.

In the same way the chief priests and the teachers of the law mocked him among themselves. "He saved others," they said, "but he can't save himself! Let this Christ, this King of Israel, come down now from the cross, that we may see and believe." Those crucified with him also heaped insults on him. (Mark 15:31– 32 NIV)

Jesus was also ridiculed by the Roman soldiers at his crucifixion as stated in Luke. "The soldiers also came up and mocked him. They offered him wine vinegar and said, 'If you are the king of the Jews, save yourself.' There was a written notice above him, which read: this is the king of the Jews" (Luke 23:37–38 NIV).

Examples of people who were ridiculed in the Bible:

• Scorned for acts of humility:

When I weep and fast, I must endure scorn; when I put on sackcloth, people make sport of me. Those who sit at the gate mock me, and I am the song of the drunkards. (Psalm 69:10– 12 NIV)

• Youth ridiculed for faith:

They have greatly oppressed me from my youth—let Israel say they have greatly oppressed me from my youth, but they have not gained the victory over me. (Psalm 129:1–2 NIV)

- Ridiculing parents:

   The eye that mocks a father, that scorns
   obedience to a mother, will be pecked out by
   the ravens of the valley, will be eaten by the
   vultures. (Proverbs 30:17 NIV)

- Wife scorned husband (Michal's contemp for David):

   But as the Ark of the Lord entered the City of
   David, Michal, the daughter of Saul, looked
   down from her window. When she saw King
   David leaping and dancing before the Lord, she
   was filled with contempt fo him.

   They brought the Ark of the Lord and set it in its
   place inside the special tent David had prepared
   for it. And David sacrificed burnt offerings
   and peace offerings to the Lord. When he had
   finished his sacrifices, David blessed the people
   in the name of the Lord of Heaven's Armies.
   Then he gave to every Israelite man and woman
   in the crowd a loaf of bread, a cake of dates, and
   a cake of raisins. Then all the people returned
   to their homes.

   When David returned home to bless his own
   family, Michal, the daughter of Saul, came
   out to meet him. She said in disgust, "How
   distinguished the king of Israel looked today,
   shamelessly exposing himself to the servant
   girls like any vulgar person might do!"

   David retorted to Michal, "I was dancing
   before the Lord, who chose me above your

father and all his family! He appointed me as the leader of Israel, the people of the Lord, so I celebrate before the Lord. Yes, and I am willing to look even more foolish than this, even to be humiliated in my own eyes! But those servant girls you mentioned will indeed think I am distinguished!" (2 Samuel 6:16–22 NLT)

- Contempt for the unfortunate:

    Men at ease have contempt for misfortune as the fate of those whose feet are slipping. (Job 12:5 NIV)

- Ridiculed on the Day of Pentecost:

    Some, however, made fun of them and said, "They have had too much wine." (Acts 2:13 NIV)

    Do not fear reproach of men. (Isaiah 51:7 NIV)

- Ridiculed prophet:

    Son of dust, your people are whispering behind your back. They talk about you in their houses and whisper about you at the doors, saying, "Come on, let's have some fun! Let's go hear him tell us what the Lord is saying!" (Ezekiel 33:30 TLB)

    Whilst the prophet was busy doing the work of God, scoffers were at their best ridiculing him.

- Youth mocking Prophet Elisha

    From there Elisha went up to Bethel. As he was walking along the road, some youths came out of the town and jeered at him. "Go on up, you baldhead!" they said. "Go on up, you baldhead!" (2 Kings 2:23 NIV)

Hear me, you who know what is right, you people who have my law in your hearts: Do not fear the reproach of men or be terrified by their insults. (Isaiah 51:7 NIV)

Reasons for ridicule:

- To show unbelief:

    But they mocked God's messengers, despised his words and scoffed at his prophets until the wrath of the Lord was aroused against his people and there was no remedy. (2 Chronicles 36:16 NIV)

- To portray scorn:

    Then King Nebuchadnezzar of Babylon came to Jerusalem and captured it, and he bound Jehoiakim in bronze chains and led him away to Babylon. Nebuchadnezzar also took some o the treasures from the Temple of the Lord, and he placed them in his palace in Babylon.

    The rest of the events in Jehoiakim's reign, including all the evil things he did and everything found against him, are recorded in The Book of the Kings of Israel and Judah. Then his son Jehoiachin became the next king.

    Jehoiachin was eighteen years old when he became king, and he reigned in Jerusalem three months and ten days. Jehoiachin did what was evil in the Lord's sight.

In the spring of the year King Nebuchadnezzar took Jehoiachin to Babylon. Many treasures from the Temple of the Lord were also taken to Babylon at that time. And Nebuchadnezzar installed Jehoiachin's uncle, Zedekiah, as the next king in Judah and Jerusalem. (2 Chronicles 36:6–10 NLT)

- To insult:

  She called her household servants. "Look," she said to them, "this Hebrew has been brought to us to make sport of us! He came in here to sleep with me, but I screamed." (Genesis 39:14–15 NIV)

  Believers can be objects of ridicule because of their faith. When you read through the book of Acts, you will realize that the believers were not only tortured but also ridiculed contemptuously. Again, in Hebrews: "Some were laughed at and their backs cut open with whips, and others were chained in dungeons" (Hebrews 11:36–37 TLB).

Rejection

To reject is to refuse to accept or acknowledge or believe in something. We throw out or discard what we believe is useless. This can apply to a thing or a person.

In biblical times, people who suffered from leprosy were rejected by society. They lived outside the community and even had to shout to announce their presence whenever they had to appear in town. In essence, those afflicted with leprosy were the rejected and were considered worthless and useless. As we remind ourselves of the meaning of rejection, we realize that, in our modern society today, many people are rejected for various reasons; for example, colour, race, tribe, physical appearance, age, economic status, political affiliation, religious or cultural beliefs, and so forth. One group of people who suffer rejection very often are children. Parental and family rejection, irresponsibility, and other issues have resulted in the large number of street children we have in the world today. A lot of these young people are bitter against their parents and society for doing little or nothing about their situation.

According to John Powell, an English composer, human beings grow in an atmosphere of acceptance and not rejection. "Human beings, like plants grow in the soil of acceptance, not in the atmosphere of rejection."[21] However, in spite of any form of rejection, Ashley Tisdale, a female American singer and producer, believes that rejection should not keep you from what you want: "Don't let anyone, or any rejection, keep you from what you want."[22]

When you allow rejection to take hold and prevent you from reaching your potential, you are likely to become bitter because of failure. This is the reason American actor, screenwriter, producer, and director Sylvester Stallone believes that rejection is a clarion call for him to wake up and get going: "I take rejection as someone blowing a bugle in my ear to wake me up and get going, rather than retreat."[23] Your rejection must be a catalyst in changing your situation for better.

> One who was there had been an invalid for
> thirty-eight years. When Jesus saw him lying
> there and learned that he had been in this

condition for a long time, he asked him, "Do you want to get well?"

"Sir," the invalid replied, "I have no one to help me into the pool when the water is stirred. While I am trying to get in, someone else goes down ahead of me." (John 5:5–7 NIV)

This man has been an invalid for thirty-eight years, and the number of years he spent around the pool trying to get his healing is not clear to me in the story. However, it is very clear that this man did not have any helper. People who are not rejected have helpers in many ways. I am inclined to think that this man had been a burden to his family and friends; therefore, they decided to dump him there and forget about him. This treatment, coupled with his inability to get into the pool when it was stirred, I believe made him a bitter person, negative in his thinking, and dwelling in the past. Jesus asked him a simple question, "Do you want to get well?" and the answer was a long winding negative story. He had been trying all this while, but had achieved no success. Rejection and failure are excellent ingredients for bitterness.

Some men came carrying a paralytic on a mat and tried to take him into the house to lay him before Jesus. When they could not find a way to do this because of the crowd, they went up on the roof and lowered him on his mat through the tiles into the middle of the crowd, right in front of Jesus. (Luke 5:18–19 NIV)

This is the story of another paralytic whose situation was different. The Bible say "some men came carrying a paralytic." Whether they were friends or family members tells me that he was not a rejected person. Could it be that, because of these men around, he had faith to believe with them for his healing?

SUPREME EXAMPLE OF REJECTION

> About the ninth hour Jesus cried with a loud voice, "Eli, Eli, lama sabachthani?" that is to say, "My God, my God, why hast thou forsaken me?" (Matthew 27:46 KJV)

> As you come to him, the living Stone—rejected by humans but chosen by God and precious to him. (1 Peter 2:4 NIV)

Jesus himself was rejected by his father at a time when Jesus was carrying the sins of the world. He was also rejected by his own people in Nazareth and the Jews in general, yet he was not bitter against anybody. You will definitely face rejection in one way or another, but that should not cause you to be angry and bitter, because you have the supreme example of our Lord to follow. It might not be easy, but there is no other choice. Your rejection should not prevent you from taking some risks to better your life.

Degeneration

WHAT IS DEGENERATION?

Degeneration is a physical, intellectual, moral, or artistic loss of power, vitality, or an essential quality that results in a worsened state or enfeeblement. It is the process of becoming worse.

From this definition we can infer that degeneration is the same as deterioration. This implies that when the life of a person begins to deteriorate, body, soul, and spirit, and he or she refuses to do something about it, or is unable to handle the rate and levels of deterioration, the likelihood of becoming angry or having a hurtful feeling is very high. There are some Christians who started as very committed, powerful in prayer, anointed and morally upright. However, due to certain circumstances they have not been able to maintain themselves and have degenerated in all these areas of their Christian life as well as life in general.

WHAT ARE SOME OF THE CAUSES OF DETERIORATION?

- **Self-justification** is one of the serious causes of deterioration in a person's life. When you measure yourself with yourself, and justify yourself as being all right, it is likely you will never progress. Here I am not talking about contentment. When you justify your mistakes as human nature, and make no attempt to deal with them, you will definitely deteriorate or degenerate in that area which you tag as "human weakness."

- **Refusing to maintain certain moral standards in life,** especially when it comes to your relationship with God and man, can result in degeneration or deterioration in the standard and quality of your life. Some people say morality is relative, but I am not talking about a "relative morality" here. I am talking about the absolute moral standards of God:

  > But just as he who called you is holy, so be holy
  > in all you do; for it is written: "Be holy, because
  > I am holy." (1 Peter 1:15–16 NIV)

  For example, in family relations, there are some norms or certain high moral standards that some families maintain. It is expected that all members of the family will abide by them. In the same way, when it comes to our relationship with God, he expects us to abide by the high moral standards he has set for his children. Maintaining these standards is not by your might or ability but by the help of his spirit and grace.

- **Maintaining certain kinds of friends, company or fellowship with unbelievers** is likely to influence to become like the people you walk with. This is clearly stated in the Bible. Evils associations corrupt good morals. That is why it is said, "show me your friend and I will show you your character."

    Do not be misled: "Bad company corrupts good character." (1 Corinthians 15:33 NIV)

A person whose life is degenerating is likely to be a bitter person, especially when he or she is envious of those who represent the standard or the truth. People who are ridiculed and rejected and whose lives are generally deteriorating easily become offended and always ready for an offensive move. They may even become jealous and envious of others whose lives are better than theirs.

Chapter 12

JEALOUSY AND THE ENVY CANKER

hen you don't have the capacity to do something, you don't have to be jealous of the one who does have it; rather, rejoice with him or her. Even if you had the capacity but God rather chose to use the other person, what business have you to be jealous or angry and bitter? You will never achieve your full potential in life when you are to preoccupied with the destruction of your so-called enemy. This is so because you will not have time to find out from God what he wants you to do for him, or even see when he is pointing to something else. This goes to prove that your vision is blurred if not completely lost, according to Astrid Alauda. She says, "I've spent most of my life walking under that hovering cloud, jealousy, whose acid raindrops blurred my vision and burned holes in my heart."[24] You will be too busy scheming to do something else to prove that you are better even though that may not be God's choice for you.

The case of King Saul and David after the war with the Philistines is a good example of what jealousy and envy can do:

> When the men were returning home after David had killed the Philistine, the women came out from all the towns of Israel to meet King Saul with singing and dancing, with joyful songs and with tambourines and lutes. As they danced, they sang: "Saul has slain his thousands, and David his tens of thousands." Saul was very angry; this refrain galled him. "They have credited David with tens of thousands," he thought, "but me with only thousands. What more can he get but the kingdom?" And from that time on Saul kept a jealous eye on David. (1 Samuel 18:6–9 NIV)

The women who came to meet the returning soldiers after the defeated the Philistines sang praises to their honour, especially for king Saul and David. Th attributions that were made to King Saul and David did not go down well with the king. This created jealousy and envy to the extent that the king wanted to kill David. Did you know that your success could be the source of your problems? The Bible says, "And from that time on Saul kept a jealous eye on David."

> Let us not become vainglorious and self-conceited, competitive and challenging and provoking and irritating to one another, envying and being jealous of one another. (Galatians 5:26 AMP)

Saul accepted the comparison that the women were making and therefore became vain and bitter. When you keep on comparing yourself to others all the time, you are very likely to dislike yourself, have a low self-esteem, and develop a bitter personality, especially if you compare yourself with those you consider better than you. If King Saul had even compared himself with the rest of the soldiers, he would have realized that he was better praised than they. He was self-conceited, unnecessarily competitive, and envious of the attention that David was receiving. The Bible says that God is a jealous God. His jealousy is to help you and me walk in holiness and to maintain a good relationship with him, which is in our own interest. But the fact that God is a jealous God does not mean that you also have the liberty to be jealous. He is sovereign.

How do you feel when somebody succeeds where you have failed? Or, if I may ask, do you feel good when someone fails? How do you feel when you compare yourself to other people? Sometimes people justify and legitimize their envy and jealousy by playing the victim. For how long can you play the victim to justify yourself?

Jealousy and envy can be found in every area of human life, but it becomes very interesting when they thrive in the church. Do you remember Korah and the others who were envious of Moses and Aaron? They ended up being destroyed. There are people in church who are envious of other people's spiritual gifts, positions in the church, and the manifestations of the Holy Spirit in others. Some are even envious of the clothes or accessories that others wear to church. You would be surprised to know that there are even pastors or "reverend" ministers who will do everything to bring down a colleague minister who is doing better than they are. I know what I am talking about. No matter your reason for being envious, it is an abomination to God.

The acts of the sinful nature are obvious: sexual immorality, impurity and debauchery; idolatry and witchcraft; hatred, discord, jealousy, fits of rage, selfish ambition, dissensions, factions and envy; drunkenness, orgies, and the like. I warn you, as I did before, that those who live like this will not inherit the kingdom of God. (Galatians 5:19–21 NIV)

Envy and jealousy are some of the acts of the flesh, and the Bible says those who live that way will not enter into heaven. Why? Here are the reasons envy and jealousy can cause you harm:

1.   They tend to make you ungrateful and unappreciative.
2.   They can make you antagonistic in your ways. Do you remember the elder brother of the prodigal son? He was jealous, angry, and antagonistic when the younger brother returned home.
3.   They can make you becom hateful and resentful
4.   They may even develop murderous tendencies in you as they did in Saul:

> You are jealous and covet [what others have] and your desires go unfulfilled; [so] you become murderers. [To hate is to murder as far as your hearts are concerned.] You burn with envy and anger and are not able to obtain [the gratification, the contentment, and the happiness that you seek], so you fight and war. You do not have, because you do not ask. (1 John 3:15 AMP)

When the envious and jealous desires, according to James, go unfulfilled, it is likely to result in murders, fights, or even war. There was once a rich man who married two wives (this is unacceptable in Christianity). In order to compensate his first wife for marrying a second woman, he set up two big shops dealing in different items and a third one, which was a restaurant because the first wife was a caterer. This woman was travelling to many places around the world buying stuff to fill her shops. The second wife was made a housewife to cater for the home and the children. Apparently the first wife was not happy because she thought the second wife was going to have more control over "things" as well as the children in the house. She wanted to be in control of the house too. She tried to talk the husband into changing that decision by giving her oversight of the house, but the husband did not agree. He wanted her to be free and available for him. In addition, the husband noticed that she was really struggling with all the businesses that he had committed to her and did not want to burden her further. This did not go down well with the woman, and therefore she began feeling bored and angry with the husband and envious of her rival. She thought her rival was better off being at home. In the course of time, she became so bitter that she found it difficult to relate to the husband, and more especially to the second wife. The situation became so bad that the second wife could not touch anything that belonged to her in the house; neither could she touch the first wife's children. Her complaints and murmurings were unending. The first wife never appreciated anything done by the second wife. There were times she was even ready to be physical with her rival. The family began to break apart as a result of this evil spirit of bitterness, but for the sake of the family, and for his own sanity and peace of mind, the man decided to divorce this woman.

So how do you deal with envy and jealousy in your life before it makes you a bitter person?

1. This may sound crazy, but is it possible to learn from the person you are envious or jealous of? After all, the reason you are envious or jealous is that the person has a certain quality or something that you don't have. It may be a skill or even looks. Try to improve your skills and do your best in everything you apply yourself to. When you do your best, then you must learn to congratulate and appreciate yourself. There is an African proverb that says, the agama lizard that fell from the tall Iroko tree praised himself when nobody did.

2. As you try to learn from this person, is it possible to put your pride and envy aside for a moment and dare appreciate him or her? What you appreciate will possibly come to you. What you don't appreciate or disregard will always move away from you.

3. Stop measuring yourself against other people; rather, seek to be thankful to God for what you are today as compared to yesterday. It does not pay to feel inferior or look down on yourself. Focus on yourself instead of others. Count your blessings once again, and you will be surprised at what the Lord has done in your life.

4. Rejoice with those who rejoice, and you will not feel envious: "Rejoice with those who rejoice; mourn with those who mourn" (Romans 12:15 NIV).

When people succeed or "make it" in reaching their goals, learn to rejoice genuinely with them. A person who lives a life of jealousy and envy is never a happy person. An unhappy person is always prone to be bitter.

Part 2

EFFECTS OF BITTERNESS

Bitterness can change your sleeping place.

Chapter 13

EIGHTEEN KILLER EFFECTS OF BITTERNESS

Bitterness always thinks and dwells on what is past. Suffocate the ugly past and bitterness will be dead. A former prime minister of Australia Sir Robert G. Menzies tells us that your joy today and the hopes you have for tomorrow can be seriously curtailed by bitterness cultivate from the past: "It is a simple but sometimes forgotten truth that the greatest enemy to present joy and high hopes is the cultivation of retrospective bitterness."[25] When bitterness has finished its work or is still at work in a person's life, there are certain effects that will be obvious or apparent. That is why American pastor Harry Emerson Fosdick said, "Bitterness imprisons life; love releases it. Bitterness paralyzes life; love empowers it. Bitterness sours life; love sweetens it. Bitterness sickens life; love heals it. Bitterness blinds life; love anoints its eyes."[26] In view of this, one cannot afford to entertain bitterness for a day.

Let me take this opportunity to discuss some of the evil effects of bitterness, knowing that I cannot exhaust completely the list of all effects.

1.   **When a person becomes bitter he or she is also likely to become a pessimist and an "enemy" of hope.**

What do I mean by this? The term *pessimism* comes from the Latin word *pessimus*, which means "worst". A pessimist is a person who, as a rule, sees the worst in everything current and anticipates the worst for the future. Because of this, a pessimist is also bound to be gloomy.

Bitterness creates a negative personality—a person who always sees and expects the worst to happen in every situation. The bitter person does not expect anything good, especially from the person or thing that caused the pain or anger in the first place. He or she does not hope for a future that is different from the status quo. What is the status quo? It is the state of acrimony, hostility and unfriendliness, the reason for revenge. The outlook of the pessimist, which is usually negative, prevails in spite of the circumstances or facts. Even though the facts may be balanced or even slightly positive, the pessimist will always look for the bad, the ugly, or the negative side of the whole issue. How can you always live your life as a pessimist? If you don't expect anything good from life, life will not give you anything good. What you don't expect you hardly prepare for. "The optimist sees the rose and not the thorns; the pessimist stares at the thorns, oblivious of the rose."[27] Kahlil Gibran. When you can only see thorns, how can you prepare for anything good?

Hope as defined by some dictionaries gives me the impression that the world's definition of hope is just a wish. The definitions include having a wish to get something or do something. It can be a wish for something to happen or for something to be true. Hope often involves something that is seen as possible or likely, and that the outcome wished for will be for the best.

The New International Dictionary of the Bible says of hope, "The biblical concept of hope is not mere expectation and desire, as in Greek literature, but includes trust and confidence in the God of hope." Hope is a necessity for every Christian, or to be precise, every human being. A lot of potential is killed when hope is lost. Hope holds on when faith has given up, but there can be no Christian hope without faith. "May the God of hope fill you with all joy and peace as you trust in him, so that you may overflow with hope by the power of the Holy Spirit" (Romans 15:13 NIV).

The bitter person as an enemy of hope finds it difficult to trust and to put his or her confidence in God. It is my prayer that the God of hope will fill you with joy and peace, which passes all understanding, so that bitterness and pessimism w ll give way to hope and optimism in your life. If you are a believer, then you have no choice but to hope in God who holds the future and has great plans for your life. Bitter people, apart from not trusting God, also usually don't trust people around them. They see almost everybody as an offender. For example, a bitter wife or husband will never hope for anything good from his or her spouse. All their expectations are negative. However, God says in Jeremiah 29:11: "'For I know the plans I have for you,' declares the Lord, 'plans to prosper you and not to harm you, plans to give you hope and a future.'" (NIV)

Christian hope is based on the confident assurance of the word of God. It is not just a wish or a feeling; rather, it is based on knowledge. In the verse above, you will notice that the Christian optimist or hopeful looks forward to the best because the word of God assures him or her that the plans of God are for his or her good. If the one who created the whole universe, who is in control of the affairs of the world no matter what happens, has plans to give you hope and a future, why should you be a pessimist? At worst you can be a "cautious optimist," if there is anything like that.

What was the hope of Absalom in the space of two years when he spoke neither good nor evil to his stepbrother, Amnon? Are you also living in the bitterness of the past, with a pessimistic outlook to life and a state of hopelessness? When a person loses hope, despair, and frustration, anxiety becomes the order of the time. Hope is very fundamental and indispensable for us to live, work, and have a meaningful existence. It's time to wake up and see how the devil is using bitterness to destroy your hope of glory. Act now!

2.   **Another dangerous effect of bitterness is that it can corrupt, damage, or alter one's faith.**

When your faith is corrupted what happens to your relationship with your God? "The thief comes only to steal and kill and destroy; I have come that they may have life, and have it to the full" (John 10:10 NIV).

This alteration or damage usually takes place when the bitter person cannot blame anybody for the changed situation. The person feels that the only person to blame, then, is God. When you begin to blame or accuse him of circumstances that you don't understand and cannot handle, the likelihood of losing your faith in him becomes great. Sometimes when tragedy hits—like the earthquake in Haiti on 12 January 2010 and the tsunami in Japan on 11 March 2011—the tendency to be bitter and blame God instead of seeking his help cannot be ruled out. When people cannot find answers in situations like these, bitterness becomes a place of refuge. What the devil is looking for in situations like these is the opportunity to destroy your faith through bitterness so he can ultimately take you to hell with him. He steals your joy and peace and sometimes even makes you emotionally unstable. He asks, if God loves you, why did he allow such a thing to happen to you? To be frank, we cannot easily answer some of these questions, but that does not change or negate the fact that God still loves you. Not even death can separate you and me from his love. (Romans 8:35)

The devil has no time for jokes. His ultimate goal is to destroy. Until you are destroyed, the purpose of bitterness will not have been achieved. That is why your anger keeps on growing, soon to become hatred, and then, with time, it will metamorphose into bitterness. At this point, you just don't hate the one who or the thing that offended you, but you hate everything and anything that person or situation represents. In the situation in which you blame God for your predicament, you may begin to hate everything that is connected to God, and if he does not show you mercy and intervene, you are likely to find yourself in a situation that you never bargained for—out of faith and out of the church. This is how far bitterness can go to destroy your faith.

Let's take another example. An abused child tends to see the abusive father in all other fathers and male figures. In the eyes of that child, they are all evil. It becomes difficult for such a person when he or she grows up to accept the love of a man or a father figure, and sometimes this is extended to any supervisor over his or her life.

The question many people often ask is, "Why did God allow this to happen to me?" Friend, you have to accept the fact that God is sovereign, and he chooses to do what he likes at any time. It is a difficult thing to swallow, but it is a fact. He loves you in spite of what you are going through. He knows the end from the beginning, and therefore knows what is best for you. Your business and my business is to trust God and seek an understanding of the situation from him. No one can question his actions. Or should I say that you can question him but he is not obliged to answer. He can also decide to wait for some time before answering you. It is his prerogative. What is important for me, and I believe for you, is that his grace, he says, is sufficient for us. He loves us so much that what concerns us concerns him. The issue of God's prerogative reminds me of the story of Noah. God gave him an assignment and directed him in carrying it out till everything was completed. When God closed the gate of the ark, as we are told in the Bible, for a long time Noah never heard from him. "The animals going in were male and female of every living thing, as God had commanded Noah. Then the Lord shut him in" (Genesis 7:16 NIV).

Take note here: it was God who shut the gate to the ark. He knew the content, but the Bible says God remembered Noah after one hundred and fifty days. Where was God? What was he doing? Did he forget about Noah? It was not because God had a memory lapse; rather, he returned when he decided to show up again. I wonder what Noah was thinking all this while? "The waters flooded the earth for a hundred and fifty days. But God remembered Noah and all the wild animals and the livestock that were with him in the ark, and he sent a wind over the earth, and the waters receded" (Genesis 7:24–8:1 NIV)

What I am trying to say is that the fact that God has not answered yet does not mean he has forgotten about you. At the appropriate time, he will show himself strong on your behalf. That is why you should not be bitter against him in any way.

When your faith is corrupted by bitterness, you will eventually cease to be fruitful in the kingdom. You will also be of no use to the kingdom's business. How can you serve a kingdom you have no belief in?

> I am the vine; you are the branches. If a man remains in me and I in him, he will bear much fruit; apart from me you can do nothing. If anyone does not remain in me, he is like a branch that is thrown away and withers; such branches are picked up, thrown into the fire and burned. If you remain in me and my words remain in you, ask whatever you wish, and it will be given you. This is to my Father's glory, that you bear much fruit, showing yourselves to be my disciples. (John 15:5–8 NIV)

You will no longer remain in him, and therefore will not bear any godly fruits. In Christ there is no bitterness, and therefore if you entertain bitterness in you, it will be impossible to produce any Christ-like characteristics. Apart from him you can do nothing. Not being in him makes it easier for the devil to attack and cut you off. Cutting you off means you will be on your own against the devil, the owner of bitterness and the controller of bitter persons. Let me remind you that, if you are not in Christ, you are no match for the devil.

3. **When you harbor bitterness for a long time, there is the likelihood that you will find it very difficult to change. Your outlook becomes "past tense." A prisoner of the past.**

I am not saying you cannot change. What I am saying is that it will not be easy. Change for many people is a difficult thing to handle. That is why sometimes it takes so long for people to accept it, especially when they cannot be sure of the long-term effect. As such, some people show their bitterness openly while others secretly keep it. Bitterness, whether secret or open, is resistant to change and friendship; it is the hallmark of selfishness. Absalom kept his bitterness secret for two years, and nobody suspected anything. He spoke neither good nor evil to the offender. One risky effect of bitterness is that it fixes your thinking and focus on the past. This is risky because it may not be too obvious to you. That is why sometimes, if it is not pointed out, you will be in the dark about it. You begin to live your life in the past, and that is why a bitter person can amazingly remember minute details of the past. When it comes to keeping records of past negative issues (especially hurts and offenses), the bitter person is very proficient. So a bitter wife or husband can remember what a spouse did ten years ago. This "past tense" outlook makes you lose focus on the future.

A woman went to discuss her problems with an elder of her church. She was concerned about how nothing she put her hands to ever succeeded. According to her, the family background was quite bad, mixed with idolatry or fetishism, and so nobody in her family ever prospered. There were no stable families or marriages. There was the belief that the family was cursed. This woman was extremely bitter with life and her forebears. When asked whether she was a believer, she responded in the affirmative. She was also asked whether she believed that Christ became a curse for her when he died on the cross. She believed. She also believed that all the deliverances she had gone through had dealt with every curse on her life, and yet this woman could not look forward to the future with any sense of hope. Her entire outlook was about the past and what had happened to her and her extended family. Her real problems were financial mismanagement and her husband's temporary unemployment challenges.

Retrospective bitterness is a sure recipe for the destruction of the joy and peace you ought to experience today. Everything you do is referenced to the past, and so you are unable to give off your best. You do whatever you do in relation to what hurt or offended you in the past. You refuse to fall in love again because you were hurt by your lover last year. You tell yourself, "If I do, what happened the last time will happen again, so why bother?" You become a prisoner of the past and refuse to open up to people or the future. Who told you that all the lovers under the sun are the same? Anyway, how many of them do you know or have you encountered? You cannot look to the future with hope for something good with this kind of attitude. Your future will be stolen from you. Here you realize that whatever hurt or offended you now has the power to overcome, control, or rule your life. You become a prisoner of the hurt or offence that has made you bitter. Your whole thinking and all your actions are premised on what made you bitter. If I may ask, what comes into your mind when you see the offender or encounter a situation that is similar to the one that made you bitter? Is there always a negative reaction?

King was reminded of the bitterness in his heart one day as he thought about his life. He thought he had forgiven Prince, a friend whom he helped to pay back someone he owed. Prince had been bound to go to prison if he failed to pay up. The deal was that Prince would pay King back in about six months, but after about eight years, the debt was still not cleared. I am not talking about a small amount in terms of that country's currency and economy. This guy had just refused to pay, and his refusal was not because he could not pay. At the time when Prince was in trouble, King and his wife did many things to help Prince's family, and yet Prince just refused to even tell them how he intended to repay this money. Just remembering this situation, according to King, makes his heart beat faster than normal, but you know he cannot go on like this forever.

Let me tell you the story of a young man who hailed from a neighbouring country who was so bitter with his mother that one day he had to sit down with her and settle the issue at the centre of it all. This young man was born out of the rape of his mother when she was in her early teens.

Out of fear, she refused to tell anybody what had happened to her. The young man, not knowing the story surrounding his birth and in his persistent effort to find out who his father was from the mother, compelled her to introduce to him a certain man as his father. The young man eventually moved in to live with this man, who already had a family in another part of town. Due to this young man's own bad character and behaviour, he was unable to live with his mother and step-father and had to move to live with the so-called father. Conditions in this new family made him believe that the man was not his real father. He never received any good treatment as a son. All this while, his life was nothing to write home about; he was really struggling to live. To make matters worse for him, one day he received a phone call from a man he did not know who claimed to be his real father. He became confused. This led him to confront his mother again, and when he pushed her hard for the truth, it became clear that the mother had lied to him concerning the so-called father he was living with. As a result of this lie, or the mother's inability to tell him the truth, this young man became very bitter against her. For years, he tried to avoid having anything to do with her. As a result of this bitterness, the young man gradually began losing control of his life. He could not look forward to the future with hope. His whole life focused on the lie the mother had told him and the suffering it had caused in his life. All he did in life was premised on "ifs": "If I had known my father, if my mother had done this and that my life would have been different." He continued to live in the past and found it very difficult to move on in life.

What was Absalom thinking about during these two years? I am pretty sure that he was thinking of what had happened in the past and how he was going to find revenge. Even if he didn't think this way constantly, I'm sure flashes of his circumstances came to him from time to time. The shearing of his sheep and the accompanying party, I believe, were greatly influenced by the bitterness he harboured against his half-brother Amnon; hence the deadly plans. Bitterness is sin, and it desires to have you as it did with Cain, Abel's brother, according to Genesis 4:7: "Sin is crouching at your door; it desires to have you." (NIV)

The Perfect is not yet come, and so there is nowhere in this world where everyone or everything is perfect. People will, by all means, make mistakes that will affect you one way or another. You may have been duped by some con man, you may have lost your partner in an accident, or a friend might have snatched your spouse from you. These things happen, and they happen to countless people all over the world. If all these people decided to brood over what happened to them and live in the bitter past, what kind of world do you think we would have? Your teenage daughter has been impregnated by a family friend. You have lost your job by a wrongful dismissal. Are you going to be bitter and hate the offenders all the days of your life? If you do not let the past go, the past will go with you, and you will end up being irrelevant to the present and the future. You don't have to end up hating everybody who has offended you and even God. Don't hurt yourself. It's about time you questioned yourself: Is there any benefit in your bitter attitude or behaviour? Does it benefit the people around or yourself?

4. **Another basic effect of bitterness is that the bitter person has the tendency to become selfish day in and day out.**

It is all about me, myself and I. This is the definition of a selfish person—one who is overly interested in himself or herself and maintains a total disregard for others. So, in other words, you can describe the same character as self-centred or self-interested. Selfishness is so dangerous that a bitter person can go to any extent to satisfy his or her selfish "need." This is what the Bible has to say in this regard: "Is it not enough for you to feed on the good pasture? Must you also trample the rest of your pasture with your feet? Is it not enough for you to drink clear water? Must you also muddy the rest with your feet?" (Ezekiel 34:18 NIV).

"So far as I am all right, I don't care what happens to the others. So far as I am in this situation of bitterness, I don't care what happens to anybody else. My interest is more important than anyone else's." These are the thoughts of a selfish person. What do you expect when this type of person is around? It is all jealousy, disorder, and all kinds of evil according to James 3:16. I am sure you do not want to be the source of evil and disorder in any environment: "For where you have envy and selfish ambition, there you find disorder and every evil practice" (James 3:16 NIV).

Bitter people, most of the time, become self-centred and myopic in their outlook because they concentrate so much on themselves and what has happened to them. Of course this does not develop in a day. For example, some rape victims, unfortunately, will shy away from society sometimes thinking they are "dirty" and responsible for what

happened even though that might not be the case. I understand that rape to a woman is like death, and therefore
when it happens, the whole interest and concentration at
that point is themselves, and rightly so. It is a matter of life
and death. However, if care is not taken, this person can be
cut off from society emotionally and physically for the rest
of her life, and fear will be the order of her life.

The young man born out of rape in the earlier story became
so engrossed with himself that he cared less about others.
He was angry with everybody and the world because everything seemed to be against him. He got a job as a teacher in
a primary school in a neighbouring country, and one day
in one of his angry moods, he beat a student mercilessly,
and that was the end of his teaching job. As I write, he
is still unemployed. On the other hand, a young woman
was raped on a university campus. The few days following the incident were not easy for her. She could not face
her friends and other students who knew her predicament.
However, when the guy who perpetrated this dastardly act
was arrested and jailed, this lady managed to forgive him
with the help of counsellors and family, and she moved on
with her life.

Irish writer Oscar Wilde wrote, "Selfishness is not living as
one wishes to live; it is asking others to live as one wishes
to live."[28] Such a selfish attitude will usually cause people
to stay away from you, thereby making you lonely both
inwardly and outwardly. Some selfish people tend to be
highly antisocial in their ways; that is, secluded and unin-
terested in the society around them. Such actions also
affect many other people, who in turn avoid them, and
in so doing cause other people to sin. They shun friend-

ship and create enemies for themselves. They hardly give, but are good receivers. They are always ready to receive sympathy for their cause. There is no blessing in this. You may lose your emotional stability and succumb to what the devil came to do under this sun as stated in John 10:10: steal, kill, and destroy your joy and peace and, if possible, your salvation.

The bitter, selfish, and self-centred person tends to rejoice at the misfortunes of others. In the story of David and Shimei in 2 Samuel 24:5–13, you will notice that, while David and his entourage were weeping as they were fleeing from Absalom, Shimei was jubilant and even cursing David in addition to all his troubles. He had a selfish interest because he thought God was avenging for his family.

5. **The root of bitterness is sin. Remaining in unconfessed sin drives away the presence of God, which is a hedge of protection around his children.**

The Bible says anyone who breaks the hedge the snake will bite: "He that diggeth a pit shall fall into it; and whoso breaketh an hedge, a serpent shall bite him" (Ecclesiastes 10:8 KJV). "Whoever digs a pit may fall into it; whoever breaks through a wall may be bitten by a snake" (Ecclesiastes 10:8 NIV).

Outside the hedge of God's protection, principles, rules, and regulations for life, the possibility of demonic attack and trouble is very high. The devil begins to have a field day since there is no opposition to his assaults. Bitterness is a spirit that is controlled by the devil to serve his purpose. If bitterness is sin, then remaining in it is courting death, both spiritual and probably physical: "For the wages of sin is death, but the gift of God is eternal life in Christ Jesus our Lord" (Romans 6:23 NIV).

The ultimate consequence of sin is death, separation from God: "'Cursed is the man who does not uphold the words of this law by carrying them out.' Then all the people shall say, 'Amen!'" (Deuter nomy 27:26 NIV).

Disobedience brings all kinds of curses upon you as stated in Deuteronomy 28 from verse 14 onwards—financial, physical, marital emotional, generational curses, and so forth (Exodus 20:5).

The psalmist says in Psalm 119:11, "I have hidden your word in my heart that I might not sin against you." (NIV).

The devil is always looking for the opportunity to attack the children of God. Being bitter paves the way and gives him the legal right to do so. Sin is his property, and therefore, where there is sin he has the right to be there. The psalmist says that hiding the word of God in his spirit or in his heart helps to keep him from sinning against God and helps to keep the devil out.

We are responsible for our sin and all its consequences. Whether somebody tempted, offended, or did anything to you does not matter here. What matters is our response, and whether God approves of it. The way you respond to hurts and offences or any other thing that makes you bitter is what makes you sin, especially when you don't realize that you are sinning. You need to repent and ask for forgiveness. You need to repent of your sin of unforgiveness.

> Some of the elders of Israel came to me and sat down in front of me. Then the word of the Lord came to me: "Son of man, these men have set up idols in their hearts and put wicked stumbling blocks before their faces. Should I let them inquire of me at all? (Ezekiel 14:1–3 NIV)

Bitterness is like an idol set up as a stumbling block in the heart of a bitter person, and this definitely becomes a barrier in your relationship with God. You cannot hold on to your bitterness like a fetish because of your desire for revenge, and expect God to give you a hearing when you call.

> When tempted, no one should say, "God is tempting me." For God cannot be tempted by evil, nor does he tempt anyone; but each one is tempted when, by his own evil desire, he is dragged away and enticed. Then, after desire has conceived, it gives birth to sin; and sin, when it is full-grown, gives birth to death. (James 1:13–15 NIV)

We are tempted by our own evil desires. The desire to seek revenge is what will make you remain in bitterness and sin. The desire to make sure the offender suffers just like you did makes forgiveness a difficult challenge. So what if the offender does not suffer the same as you hope for until you or the offender dies? Are you saying that you will remain in bitterness and risk hell? God forbid!

The following story is not scientifically proven; however, I believe it will help us to rethink the subject of bitterness. I am told of a lady who was declared dead in a hospital. After some time, she came back to life, and according to her she had gone to heaven when she died. This was her testimony to the fellowship she belonged to. On entering a first gate in heaven, no one asked her any questions, but just as she was about to enter a second gate, she was told to go back because she was not fit or ready for heaven, the reason being that she was harbouring a lot of bitterness in her heart. Her return from heaven saw her come back to life in the health facility. After her discharge from the hospital, she sought help to deal with the issue of bitterness. She was counselled and received help to deal with the root of bitterness by forgiving and reconciling with some people. Sadly, after about a month she died "again" and was buried. As to where she went, only God can tell.

> Not everyone who says to me, "Lord, Lord," will enter the kingdom of heaven, but only he who does the will of my Father who is in heaven. (Matthew 7:21 NIV)

> For from within, out of men's hearts, come evil thoughts, sexual immorality, theft, murder, adultery, greed, malice, deceit, lewdness, envy, slander, arrogance and folly. All these evils come from inside and make a man "unclean." (Mark 7:21–23 NIV)

Jesus said all evil emanates from the heart including bitterness. You are defiled by any root of bitterness (Hebrews 12:15). "Another man dies in bitterness of soul, never having enjoyed anything good" (Job 21:25 NIV).

The bitter person can die in his or her bitterness without enjoying the goodness that God has for him or her. God's plans for you are for good and not for evil. There is so much to enjoy in life, so why do you confine yourself to the bitterness of your bitterness? Get out of the selfish cell in the prison of bitterness and experience a better life. Don't lose your blesings.

6. **Becoming infected with bitterness might make you whine, complain, murmur, and sometimes gossip as you try to justify yourself.**

You may also have low self-esteem. The bitter person may talk to anyone who will listen to his or her side of the story, which is very likely meant to justify him or herself.

"Therefore I will not keep silent; I will speak out in the anguish of my spirit, I will complain in the bitterness of my soul" (Job 7:11 NIV). Job, in the bitterness of his soul, became a complaining person as a result of his problems, and that is what many bitter persons tend to do. You have every right to complain: Yes, you are angry or in pain, but how does that add anything good to your situation? It makes it worse and colours your perceptions seriously. In the worst situation you may cease to be objective. Everything you get involved in becomes subjective in relation to your bitter situation. A bitter spouse in a marriage is one of the most difficult persons to live with. Love vanishes from the relationship and it becomes a matter of endurance.

When the God factor is removed from your suffering, you are left with nothing but bitterness and complaining. When you allow God to take the centre stage in your pain or suffering or anything which has made you bitter, it will not be easy for you to complain or murmur all the time because you will know that God is involved.

> Anyone who hides hatred is a liar. Anyone who spreads gossip is a fool. (Proverbs 10:18 GNT)

> They sharpen their tongues like swords and aim their words like deadly arrows. (Psalm 64:3 NIV)

When bitterness is not dealt with, the tendency to become a gossip and to go around saying deadly things about the offender and what he or she represents, becomes very real. Your tongue becomes like a sword slaughtering and assassinating people or organizations.

7.   **The bitter person makes nonsense of the grace of God in that he or she behaves as if there is nothing like forgiveness in God.**

> Therefore, the Kingdom of Heaven can be compared to a king who decided to bring his accounts up to date with servants who had borrowed money from him. In the process, one of his debtors was brought in who owed him millions of dollars. He couldn't pay, so his master ordered that he be sold—along with his wife, his children, and everything he owned—to pay the debt.

> But the man fell down before his master and begged him, "Please, be patient with me, and I will pay it all." Then his master was filled with pity for him, and he released him and forgave his debt.

But when the man left the king, he went to a fellow servant who owed him a few thousand dollars. He grabbed him by the throat and demanded instant payment.

His fellow servant fell down before him and begged for a little more time. "Be patient with me, and I will pay it," he pleaded. But his creditor wouldn't wait. He had the man arrested and put in prison until the debt could be paid in full.

When some of the other servants saw this, they were very upset. They went to the king and told him everything that had happened. Then the king called in the man he had forgiven and said," You evil servant! I forgave you that tremendous debt because you pleaded with me. Shouldn't you have mercy on your fellow servant, just as I had mercy on you?" Then the angry king sent the man to prison to be tortured until he had paid his entire debt.

That's what my heavenly Father will do to you if you refuse to forgive your brothers and sisters from your heart. (Matthew 18:23–3 NLT)

As illustrated by this story, the bitter person has no heart for forgiveness. Forgiving is a difficult thing to do, but if you can realize that you have been forgiven much, you will think again and again before holding somebody's offense against him or her. Do you know how much you have been forgiven and are being forgiven every day? Friend, there is grace, and the sooner you recognize and accept that, the better it will be for you.

A friend who was going to have a wedding in a few weeks' time just happened to meet up with me after work one day in our church car park. In our discussion, I mentioned to him that I was writing a book on bitterness. He laughed, shook his head, and asked me if I had ever been bitter before. He began to tell me about an experience he'd had that morning. He received a call from a person he had hated and born a grudge against for a long time. This person had heard that this young man was going to have a wedding and that he was ready to release his car for the wedding activities. All this while the young man telling me the story thought he was all right with that person so far as he had nothing to do with him. To his surprise, he reacted so badly he realized that he had not forgiven that person, and this led us to discuss what he could do. He realized that he was denying himself of the grace of God and his peace.

What, then, is grace? Grace is all the good things that God has given us out of his nature as the God of grace even though we don't deserve it. So, if God has given us all the good things in spite of who we are, then I think you will be better off if you accept grace for yourself and extend it to the one who hurt or offended you.

> Yet he was merciful; he forgave their iniquities
> and did not destroy them. Time after time he
> restrained his anger and did not stir up his full
> wrath. He remembered that they were but flesh,
> a passing breeze that does not return. (Psalm
> 78:38–39 NIV)

Whatever we have is by grace, and not by our abilities and skills or connections. To be forgiven is a grace of God, and without it we are doomed for hell. If God in his mercy forgives us when we confess our sins and repent, who are you or who am I, then, to hold the sin or offence of another against him or her? Even just the fact that you have life shows the grace of God on you. It is just by grace that you have been saved and that you can call yourself a child of God. I believe we all can become unforgiving from time to time, but the danger is in holding on to unforgiveness for a long time, and becoming an anger nurse, lending yourself to the spirit of bitterness.

> For it is by grace you have been saved, through faith—and this not from yourselves, it is the gift of God—not by works, so that no one can boast. (Ephesians 2:8–9 NIV)

> God made him who had no sin to be sin for us, so that in him we might become the righteousness of God. (2 Corinthians 5:21 NIV)

Christ did not have to die on the cross. He did nothing wrong that would make it necessary for him to pay with his life. He did this so that you and I could obtain the righteousness of God. A bitter person is unforgiving, and that is the root of all bitterness. *Unforgiveness!* Bitterness makes you take you eyes off the grace of God to focus only on how he has "let you down" or how others have offended you.

"He would crush me with a storm and multiply my wounds for no reason" (Job 9:17 NIV). Job at this point in his suffering was seeing God as unforgiving. His suffering was such that he thought God was punishing him for his sins without mercy. Our God is a merciful God, and at the same time just. The Bible tells us that his mercy endures forever, and this should assure you and me that his grace is always there for us if only we will accept it.

> If you forgive anyone, I also forgive him. And what I have forgiven—if there was anything to forgive—I have forgiven in the sight of Christ for your sake, in order that Satan might not outwit us. For we are not unaware of his schemes. (2 Corinthians 2:10–11 NIV)

Satan gains an advantage in every bitter situation because that is his territory. He is more skilful in it than you are. The only way you can beat him to it is to let him take his thing away from you. As long as you hold on to it, he will definitely outwit you.

> Make every effort to live in peace with all men and to be holy; without holiness no one will see the Lord. See to it that no one misses the grace of God and that no bitter root grows up to cause trouble and defile many. (Hebrews 12:14–16 NIV)

You need holiness to see God. Bitterness is a barrier to holiness and will only bring you trouble and defilement.

"Anyone who hates his brother is a murderer, and you know that no murderer has eternal life in him" (1 John 3:15 NIV). This is scary and hard to accept. The bitter person definitely hates the person who offended him or her. For this person, grace does not exist, and therefore, the only solution is revenge or ill will for the offender. The Bible says such a person is a murderer and does not have eternal life. This is serious, and that is why you have to do all in your power with the help of the Holy Spirit to overcome bitterness.

> They made their hearts as hard as flint and would not listen to the law or to the words that the Lord Almighty had sent by his Spirit through the earlier prophets. So the Lord Almighty was very angry. (Zechariah 7:12 NIV)

> Thus you nullify the word of God by your tradition that you have handed down. And you do many things like that. (Mark 7:13 NIV)

What is this tradition? It is the status quo of bitterness and acrimony that will not listen to godly counsel. Bitterness nullifies the word of God. "Teach me to do your will, for you are my God; may your good Spirit lead me on level ground" (Psalm 143:10 NIV).

May the good Holy Spirit o God lead you to where you ought to be as a child of God.

8.   Bitterness could be the cause of some diseases.

Bitterness is a spiritual poison that causes stress, which produces actual toxins in the body. It creates unnecessary fear and anxiety, which can increase one's blood pressure, elevate one's heart rate, thus inducing an increased risk of heart disease. You can develop stomach ulcers as a result of eating disorders that come about due to fear and anxiety. Bitterness makes physical healing more difficult because spiritual healing may be needed before physical healing can happen. But when you doubt God, how can you receive spiritual healing? Bitterness is poison to your body, soul, and spirit. It makes you sin, and sin makes you feel depressed, reducing your productivity and energy levels. It may cause headaches and drain your vitality, thus making you unable to achieve your full potential.

9. **Bitterness, whose root is unforgiveness, has the capacity to create a chain of sins.**

The first sin I can think of is self-pity. Self-pity is self-induced misery. Feeling sorry for oneself is the outcome of a self-indulgent attitude and a selfish focussing on one's hardships and difficulties.

American author and political activist Helen Keller wrote, "Self-pity is our worst enemy and if we yield to it, we can never do anything wise in this world."[29] I don't think this is an overstatement at all because it puts you in a situation where nothing seems to hold in your life. This is reinforced by Winifred Rhoades who says, "To feel sorry for oneself is one of the most disintegrating things the individual can do to himself.[30] It is a dangerous situation as shown in this anonymous quote: "Self-pity is one of the most dangerous forms of self-centeredness. It fogs our vision."[31]

Effects of self-pity

Cain said to the Lord, "My punishment is more than I can bear. Today you are driving me from the land, and I will be hidden from your presence; I will be a restless wanderer on the earth, and whoever finds me will kill me." (Genesis 4:13–14 NIV)

One of the effects of self-pity is cruelty. Shimei was one whose self-pity caused him to curse David on his way to exile and never have any sympathy for him. His open cursing of David set a bad example for the people of Israel, and this likely affected many.

Self-pity also leads to self-justification for all the wrongs in one's life. Some people love to feel sorry for themselves so they can justify why they do the evil things prevailing in their lives. For example, a kleptomaniac may cry every time he or she is arrested and say, "I feel sorry for myself. I can't help it." An unfaithful husband may use self-pity to justify his infidelity. He could weep over it before his wife but not really be ready to deal with it. A person who indulges in self-pity may enjoy the result because he or she may be receiving sympathy from sympathizers.

From the quotes I have mentioned, you will notice that self-pity can interfere with right thinking. You hardly can see clearly due to the concentration on your pitiful situation. You have to determine in your heart and mind to get rid of self-pity; otherwise, it will get rid of you.

> "See to it that no one falls short of the grace of God and that no bitter root grows up to cause trouble and defile many" (Hebrew 12:15 NIV, emphasis mine).

The Bible categorically warns that one's sins can cause other people to sin. God will not take kindly to this. Antagonism, lack of love, unbelief, defiance, and disobedience to the word of God are sometimes the effects of self-pity.

10. **The bitter person could possibly miss the grace of God.**

Whilst you refuse to accept that the grace of God is there for the offender or the one who hurt you, you may also not be able to accept that grace for yourself either. On the other hand, if you accept the grace for yourself but deny it for the offender, then there is a different problem.

> See to it that no one falls short of the grace of God and that no bitter root grows up to cause trouble and defile many. (Hebrews 12:15–16 NIV)

> You stiff-necked people! Your hearts and ears are still uncircumcised. You are just like your ancestors: You always resist the Holy Spirit! (Acts 7:51 NIV)

Don't resist the Holy Spirit and risk missing the grace of the Lord for your life. God's grace is there for all, but it is a choice. He does not force it on anybody. Choose to be a beneficiary, and allow the offender also to benefit.

11. **You may become obsessed and troubled, and this can lead ultimately to spiritual death.**

Bitterness can create an idol out of an offender because of vengeance. You become too focused and fixated on the offender for revenge, or at best, an apology. You become a prisoner of revenge, locked up in thoughts about the offender.

When you are obsessed with your bitterness, you never develop beyond the emotional level at which you were hurt. In other words, your level of tolerance will remain the same until you learn to forgive. Bitterness is like emotional suicide. It is said that bitterness is like drinking poison and expecting the offender or the one who hurt you to die. The bitter emotion is in you, not in the other person. Both Cain and Absalom became obsessed with their anger, which led to Cain's banishment and Absalom's death eventually. The best example so far as this issue is concerned is the story of a very highly placed government official in Persia called Haman in the Bible. Haman plotted to kill Mordecai:

> When Haman left the banquet he was happy and in a good mood. But then he saw Mordecai at the entrance of the palace, and when Mordecai did not rise or show any sign of respect as he passed, Haman was furious w th him. But he controlled himself and went on home. Then he invited his friends to his house and asked his wife Zeresh to join them. He boasted to them about how rich he was, how many sons he had, how the king had promoted him to high office, and how much more important he was than any of the king's other officials. "What is more," Haman went on, "Queen Esther gave a banquet for no one but the king and me, and we are invited back tomorrow. But none of this means a thing to me as long as I see that Jew Mordecai sitting at the entrance of the palace." (Esther 5:9–13 GNT)

This man was filled with bitterness and rage, and had no satisfaction in spite of all his possessions and position. His obsession to destroy the Jews made him construct gallows for their execution, which unfortunately became his own death instrument. The progression of his obsession can be found in Esther 3:5–6, 13 and 5:14. The gallows were initially made for Mordecai; however, the idea changed to include all the Jews.

12. **Bitterness creates enmity between people.**

It is not at all interesting to live with or be around some-one who is bitter. A bitter person is sometimes quite dis-agreeable, and it is not easy to enjoy his or her company. Bitter people are hardly team players. Can you imagine a married couple who are bitter against each other, and yet live under the same roof? Nothing meaningful hap-pens between them. Imagine a sales team comprised of members who are bitter against each other. People are not ready to risk rejection from bitter people; they there-fore shun their company. Bitter people may not invest in the people around them. They will not take the first step to make friends, but may at the same time expect others to reach out and sympathize with them. They deprive themselves of the opportunities that come with friendship. All those who are friends to their enemies are also enemies. There is a saying: "To have a friend, be a friend." Absalom created enmity between him and his siblings with his state of bitterness.

> Two are better than one, because they have a good return for their work: If one falls down, his friend can help him up. But pity the man who falls and has no one to help him up! Also, if two lie down together, they will keep warm. But how can one keep warm alone? Though one may be overpowered, two can defend themselves. A cord of three strands is not quickly broken. (Ecclesiastes 4:9–12 NIV)

It is harder to win back the friendship of an offended brother than to capture a fortified city. His anger shuts you out like iron bars. (Proverbs 18:19 TLB)

When bitterness creates enmity between people, it is also likely that the individuals will become reactionary to each other and other people's initiatives and also likely to oppose anything that is critical of them, even if it is constructive criticism. They will be very sensitive to criticism and will always be thinking about whatever is said is about them. This is a barrier to progress in life, and as Mother Teresa of Calcutta has it, "If you judge people, you have no time to love them."[32]

13. **In the case where the bitterness is a result of jealousy and envy, the bitter person may lose focus and miss the purpose of God for his or her life.**

Saul spent his time chasing David and not achieving much for the nation, the reason why God made him a king. That is why God said he had regretted making him a king. You may be working in an office where you feel quite bitter about your boss. No matter what he did, with bitterness in your heart, how do you expect to do your work well and be promoted? Who has to do the recommendation for your promotion? Spiritually and relationally, you have put a cloud of iron over your head, and therefore there will be no room for growth. You will look stupid and ignorant in the sight of God due to the fact that, in his plans, he may have marked you for something great, but due to bitterness you are unable to see what he has put in place for you. "Then I realized how bitter I had become, how pained I had been by all I had seen.

I was so foolish and ignorant—I must have seemed like a senseless animal to you" (Psalm 73:21–22 NLT).

14. **One of the evil effects of bitterness is that your offerings become an abomination to the Lord.**

> Your offerings become unacceptable to the Lord until the right thing is done.
>
> But I tell you that anyone who is angry with his brother will be subject to judgment. Again, anyone who says to his brother, "Raca," is answerable to the Sanhedrin. But anyone who says, 'You fool!' will be in danger of the fire of hell.
>
> Therefore, if you are offering your gift at the altar and there remember that your brother has something against you, leave your gift there in the front of the altar. First go and be reconciled to your brother; then come and offer your gift. (Matthew 5:22–24 NIV)

You may argue that this scripture refers to a situation in which you are the offender, but the fact is, so far as there is enmity represented by bitterness in your relationship, you will need to act to settle the matter. Until there is reconciliation and peace, the offering is unacceptable. It does not matter how fat it is. This is hard truth. Lord help us!

15. **The most dangerous effect of bitterness to me is that it is a serious hindrance to prayer.**

You cannot hold on to bitterness and expect your prayers to be answered. Bitterness is a hindrance to prayer. It does no matter how long you fast and pray, it will not amount to anything. When your prayer is not "reaching" God as a result of sin, you also create a doorway for enemy attack. "If I had cherished sin in my heart, the Lord would not have listened" (Psalm 66:18 NIV)

Can you imagine a couple who are bitter against each other, or even a couple in which only one of them is bitter against the other? The family would be in trouble. The devil will be having a field day with this family of confusion and pain. There is a couple who live in an uncompleted building. This couple fight so often that I sometimes wonder whether they had any relationship before the marriage or coming to live together. When they fight, the sort of things they say to each other is unprintable. They are so bitter with each other that I wonder what their two kids are learning from them. If you are bitter against your spouse, please pause here and reflect on the things that are happening in the family. Are you happy about them?

Are you a senior pastor who is bitter with your associates or church members who hurt you some time ago? Have you sat down to reflect on the happenings in your church of late? Do you understand why the numbers are dwindling in your church, and why the anointing is no more manifest?

Do you know why you are no more interested in prayer? Could it be that bitterness has choked out your love for communicating with God? Please reflect.

16. Bitterness steals the joy and peace of the Lord from your heart.

If you are really a Christian, you will never know peace and joy in your heart until you settle whatever issue caused your bitterness. If you are normal and feel happy in your bitterness, then there is something wrong somewhere. The devil's agenda is to make you unhappy, so if you give him the chance by holding onto the jealously that is in his arsenal, he will encourage you to do so. "The thief's purpose is to steal, kill and destroy" (John 10:10 TLB).

17. Bitterness will deny you the right to be an imitator of God.

Be imitators of God, therefore, as dearly loved children and live a life of love, just as Christ loved us and gave himself up for us as a fragrant offering and sacrifice to God. (Ephesians 5:1–2 NIV)

You are commanded or entreated to imitate God, but how can you imitate God with bitterness in your heart? God is a God of love, and as children of God we are supposed to live a life of love, imitating God. A bitter heart will not permit this. If you don't imitate God, you are likely to imitate the devil. That is why the bitter person can rejoice at the calamity of someone who offended him or her. This is a very wicked thing, and God certainly takes notice of such behaviour, especially if it is one of his children.

Be very careful, then, how you live—not as unwise but as wise, making the most of every opportunity, because the days are evil. Therefore do not be foolish, but understand what the Lord's will is. (Ephesians 5:15–18 NIV)

18. **Bitterness will kill your anointing.**

> But the anointing which you have received from Him abides in you, and you do not need that anyone teach you; but as the same anointing teaches you concerning all things, and is true, and is not a lie, and just as it has taught you, you will abide in Him. (1 John 2:27 NKJV)

You can remain in the anointing only when you remain in him, and how can you remain in him when you are full of bitterness and not ready to give it up? Saul lost his anointing when his focus changed as a result of bitterness against David. It was the result of shifting from the assignment God had given him to focus on David, his so-called archenemy.

Let the anointing teach you about all things, including the renewing of your mind so as to enable you to present yourself as a living sacrifice, holy and acceptable unto the Lord, free from the poison of bitterness.

> Do you not know that you are the temple of God and that the Spirit of God dwells in you? If anyone defiles the temple of God, God will destroy him. For the temple of God is holy, which temple you are. (1 Corinthians 3:16–17 NKJV)

The Bible tells us that our bodies, as Christians, are temples of God and that the Holy Spirit lives in us. This is wonderful. The place where the spirit of God lives is a holy place and must be kept as such. How then can the Holy Spirit and the unholy spirit of bitterness live in the same place? There are many Christians today who acknowledge that they are born again and filled with the Holy Spirit. They speak in great tongues that sometimes even "confuse" angels, showing themselves outwardly as very pious. However, some of these same people are so much filled with bitterness, rancour, and evil thoughts that you ask yourself if there is an inconsistency here.

> Woe to you, tea hers of the law and Pharisees, you hypocrites! You clean the outside of the cup and dish, but inside they are full of greed and self-indulgence. Blind Pharisee! First clean the inside of the cup and dish, and then the outside also will be clean.

> Woe to you, teachers of the law and Pharisees, you hypocrites! You are like whitewashed tombs, which look beautiful on the outside but on the inside are full of dead men's bones and everything unclean. In the same way, on the outside you appear to people as righteous but on the inside you are full of hypocrisy and wickedness. (Matthew 23:25–28 NIV)

This scripture in which Jesus rebukes the Pharisees for their hypocrisy tells me that it is very dangerous to entertain evil in your holy body where the Holy Spirit dwells. Rather, it is more important to make sure the holy temple of God is kept holy than it is to appear to people as righteous. Anything that is unholy should not be allowed in the holy temple of God. How can bitterness and the joy of the Lord live in the same place? Bitterness and the anointing are incompatible. It is like a believer being unequally yoked with an unbeliever. Anyone who defiles the temple of God, the Bible says, God will destroy. For the temple of God is holy, which you are.

All these effects of bitterness on a person's life tell us that bitterness is not something to joke with. It will confiscate all your blessings, or assets. It will **imprison your mind**, if not your very personality. You must either destroy it, or it will destroy you.

Now, having identified some of the effects of bitterness on a person's life, we can create a summary of the character profile of a bitter person, pointing out symptoms of bitterness. I hope this will help us to see what we are dealing with at a glance. To review, the bitter person is:

1. **Resentful** – Resentful people are annoyed about having been badly treated. They are resentful towards whatever offended them and, if they perceive God as the culprit or the offender, they begin to cut him off. They get to the place where they no more can be advised or asked to forgive. They do not care about the word of God anymore and therefore begin to walk in disobedience. They also do not care about the one they are bitter against. Disobedience, the Bible says, is like the sin of witchcraft.

2. **Rancorous** – Rancorous people deeply hold a bitter resentment and wishes of ill will that can last a long time.

3. **Hostile** – Hostile people are highly unfriendly and show feelings of hatred, enmity, antagonism, or anger toward those they think have caused them ill will. These are not team players. They oppose everything and are very critical of others. They hardly see any good in anybody. They are not ready to forgive; rather, they hold grudges.

4. **Sulky** – Sulky people are harbouring silent anger and resentment over a real or perceived grievance. They are often in a bad mood and refuse to communicate..

5. **Acrimonious** – Acrimonious people display resentful and angry behaviour. They are use to help anyone and sometimes complain when given the opportunity to help.

6. **Disagreeable** – Disagreeable people are unpleasant to be around. They are discourteous and quarrelsome and often look for reasons to disagr e with others.

7. **Frustrated** – Frustrated people feel exasperated, discouraged, or unsatisfied as well as totally ungrateful. They tend to be sensitive to everything around them and can be paranoid, thinking everything and everyone is against them.

Part 3

SOLUTIONS

....

All the solutions lie with you.

Chapter 14

HOW TO AVOID BEING BITTER

Allow me to use this cliché: "prevention is better than cure" and on this score English cleric Henry de Bracton agrees with me when he wrote in the 13th century, "An ounce of prevention is worth a pound of cure."[33] This is why I want to deal with the prevention of bitterness before going on to the cure. If you are able to prevent the bird from making its nest on your head, there will be no need getting rid of any nest. Getting rid of bitterness may be more difficult than preventing it.

Do you know who you are in Christ? You are a better person than what bitterness wants to portray you to be. If you know who you are, then it should not be too difficult for you to avoid getting into a state of bitterness. If I may ask, whose are you?

> You have been raised to life with Christ, so set
> your hearts on the things that are in heaven,
> where Christ sits on his throne at the right side

of God. Keep your minds fixed on things there, not on things here on earth. For you have died, and your life is hidden with Christ in God. Your real life is Christ and when he appears, then you too will appear with him and share his glory! (Colossians 3:1–17 NIV)

The Old Life and the New

You must put to death, then, the earthly desires at work in you, such as sexual immorality, indecency, lust, evil passions, and greed (for greed is a form of idolatry).[34] Because of such things God's anger will come upon those who do not obey him. At one time you yourselves used to live according to such desires, when your life was dominated by them.

But now you must get rid of all these things: anger, passion, and hateful feelings. No insults or obscene talk must ever come from your lips. Do not lie to one another, for you have put off the old self with its habits and have put on the new self. This is the new being which God, its Creator, is constantly renewing in his own image, in order to bring you to a full knowledge of himself. As a result, there is no longer any distinction between Gentiles and Jews, circumcised and uncircumcised, barbarians, savages, slaves, and free, but Christ is all, Christ is in all.

You are the people of God; he loved you and chose you for his own. So then, you must clothe yourselves with compassion, kindness, humility, gentleness, and patience. Be tolerant with one another and forgive one another whenever any of you has a complaint against someone else. You must forgive one another just as the Lord has forgiven you. And to all these qualities add love, which binds all things together in perfect unity. The peace that Christ gives is to guide you in the decisions you make; for it is to this peace that God has called you together in the one body. And be thankful. Christ's message in all its richness must live in your hearts. Teach and instruct one another with all wisdom. Sing psalms, hymns, and sacred songs; sing to God with thanksgiving in your hearts. Everything you do or say, then, should be done in the name of the Lord Jesus, as you give thanks through him to God the Father. (Colossians 3:1–17 GNT)

Child of God, the Bible says you have been raised with Christ and seated with him in heavenly places at the right hand of God. Therefore, set your mind on things above, and in so doing you will realize that bitterness has no place in your life. This means that you should focus your affection on godly things and put God first in everything you do. "But seek first his kingdom and his righteousness and all these things will be given to you as well" (Matthew 6:33).

Your life, child of God, is also now hidden with Christ in God. In verse 12 of Colossians 3 the word of God clearly says that you have been chosen by God. You have been made holy by him, and you are loved so dearly that anything that is incompatible with these things must be taken out of your life immediately when they rear their ugly heads.

Blessed are the merciful, for they will be shown mercy. (Matthew 5:7 NIV)

But you are a chosen people, a royal priesthood, a holy nation, a people belonging to God, that you may declare the praises of him who called you out of darkness into his wonderful light. Once you were not a people, but now you are the people of God; once you had not received mercy, but now you have received mercy. (1 Peter 2:9–10 NIV)

What a message in the Word! What grace! What did you and I do to deserve this? Nothing! This is the reason why you cannot, and should not, allow the devil to change your status in Christ with bitterness.

So what should you do to avoid being bitter?

1. **Learn to forgive those who sin against you and also forgive yourself immediately or as soon as possible for the wrong decisions or actions you have taken that could ruin your life.**

This must be done immediately as soon as you become aware of your anger and hurt. Sometimes it is very easy to forgive, but other times it is not. However, friend, if you want to remain in Christ and enjoy your status in him, then you have no option but to forgive and let go. Jesus himself set an example for us to follow. When he was being crucified he looked at the people who were driving the cruel nails and those who said "crucify him" as ignorant people who did not know what they were doing. Is it possible for you and me to give the benefit of the doubt to the offender? If we are able to do this immediately, I am sure bitterness will not be able to take root in our lives. If it worked with Jesus, who now lives his life through you, then it is also possible with you. Show mercy by your forgiveness. Hallelujah!

One day Peter went to Jesus and asked him a question about forgiveness and Jesus gave a very interesting answer. This can be found in Matthew 18:21–22:

> Then Peter came to Jesus and asked "Lord, how many times shall I forgive my brother or sister who sins against me? Up to seven times?" Jesus answered, "I tell you, not seven times, but seventy-seven times. (NIV)

I am sure Peter was thinking, if it is seven times then that must be "cool." But he was in for a shocker. Jesus told him seventy times seven, effectively saying 490 times (meaning many times), and I am inclined to believe that applies to only one person—one offender. You and I have a lot of forgiving to do. Unforgiveness is like a yoyo. A yoyo does not move by itself. The moment you stop pulling it, it begins to lose its momentum; after a while, it stops moving. Decide to forgive. It may not happen immediately, but so far as you have decided to do so and keep on affirming your intention, it will surely happen. American businessman Paul Boese wrote, "Forgiveness does not change the past, but it does enlarge the future."[2] the past is gone but the future can be enlarged or constricted by your forgiveness or unforgiveness.

Have you ever said the Lord's Prayer before? Do you recall this phrase: "And forgive us our trespasses as we forgive those who trespass against us"? What do you think? "And when you stand praying, if you hold anything against any-one, forgive him, so that your Father in heaven may for-give you your sins" (Mark 11:25 NIV).

Why is it difficult to forgive sometimes?

- It is not possible to forgive and forget completely and begin to trust the offender again immediately. I have heard people say, "forgive and forget." I wonder if any normal human being can completely forget what a wicked per-son has done to him or her. Can you forget someone who shot and almost killed you? It is impossible to forget, but possible to forgive such a person. The fact that you still remember is not grounds for bitterness or revenge. This issue of not forgetting is a fact of life, especially if you were deeply hurt. If somebody mentions the name of the person who hurt you, can you tell me that you will not remember what the person did or did not do? Anyway, trust has to be earned if you have to trust the offender again.

- It may also be that you are afraid that, if the offender does not suffer any punishment for his or her offence, he or she may repeat it.

- It is also possible that you enjoy the bitter feeling you have, especially when you see the offender and you express yourself to your satisfaction. There are people who can beat their chests and declare themselves as first-class or platinum litigants.

- Because the devil knows that unforgiveness makes you weak against him, he will do everything to encourage or help you find "a million" reasons for not forgiving. That is why you can stay up the whole night planning how you will take revenge without blinking an eye, but try to pray for just thirty minutes of the night, and it will be another story altogether.

What are the facts of true or genuine forgiveness?

- Know that forgiveness is a process. It is not a one-time event achieved by simply saying, "I forgive you." Neither is it a matter of shaking hands after a conflict and thinking that will resolve everything. Sometimes you have to keep on reminding yourself that you have forgiven the offender.

- You help yourself when you forgive the offender. You don't do the offender as much of a favour by forgiving as you do for yourself. Wha you are doing is breaking the power of the offender over your life. You free yourself from that controlling force. Forgiveness gives you power over the offender. Jesus advised us to do good to our enemies, and by so doing we heap coals of fire on their heads.

  > Therefore if thine enemy hunger, feed him; if he thirst, give him drink: for in so doing thou shalt heap coals of fire on his head. Be not overcome of evil, but overcome evil with good. (Romans 12:20–21 KJV)

- You should see offence as a steppingstone and not a stumbling block. Refuse to give yourself to the offender to take you through all the effects of an offence. The offender is not worthy of that. This is why Jesus, in love, forgave those who were crucifying him. He would not allow the offence to lead him to sin and deprive him the glory of saving mankind. Don't be like Absalom who allowed bitterness to control him for two solid years.

- True forgiveness is letting go of the pain that you suffered or are suffering as a result of hurt or offence. This letting go breaks the desire for revenge. This takes time and constant practice. Sometimes you may have to talk audibly to yourself declaring your forgiveness. It can be a struggle, but you should not give up. Fight the desire for revenge with all seriousness until you achieve it.

- True forgiveness will always seek the help of God. Plead the blood of Jesus so that the purpose of the offence will not be accomplished.

- Acknowledge that you are hurt. It may even be good to talk to the person who caused the pain. Explain how you are hurt or offended by what happened or did not happen, what was said or was omitted. If it doesn't work, don't pretend everything is all right. Seek help from godly counsellors or your pastor. Never go to the altar of God with unforgiveness in your heart. Pray for the ability to let go offences and hurt feelings.

- You may not have to go to the offender and tell him or her you have forgiven the offence. Let it be in your heart and other actions. Going to the offender may even hurt you more when the atmosphere and timing are not right. Can you imagine how you would feel and how your face would look if you were to go to the offender only to hear, "I don't know what you are talking about. I thought you rather offended me!" or "I don't see anything wrong with what I did."

- True forgiveness does not wait for an apology. It may never come. You will be hurting yourself all the more. It is not your duty to insist on an apology from the offender. (That's weird, eh!) Yours is to forgive. You will not be forgiven if you don't forgive.

> For if you forgive men when they sin against you, your heavenly Father will also forgive you. But if you do not forgive men their sins, your Father will not forgive your sins. (Matthew 6:14–15 NIV)

- True forgiveness looks to the cross because it deals with every form of injustice. God will settle it all for you. Vengeance is the Lord's:"

> And when you stand praying, if you hold anything a ainst anyone, forgive him, so that your Father in heaven may forgive you your sins. (Mark 11:25 NIV)

2. Walk in love to avoid bitterness.

> Jesus replied: "Love the Lord your God with all your heart and with all your soul and with all your mind." This is the first and greatest commandment. And the second is like it: "Love your neighbor as yourself." All the Law and the Prophets hang on these two commandments. (Matthew 22:37–40 NIV)

> My command is this: Love each other as I have loved you. (John 15:12–13 NIV)

> He who covers and forgives an offense seeks love, but he who repeats or harps on a matter separates even close friends. (Proverbs 17:9 AMP)

Hatred stirs up dissension, but love covers over all wrongs. (Proverbs 10:12 NIV)

Love is patient and kind; it is not jealous or conceited or proud; love is not ill-mannered or selfish or irritable; love does not keep a record of wrongs; love is not happy with evil, but is happy with the truth. Love never gives up; and its faith, hope, and patience never fail. Love is eternal. There are inspired messages, but they are temporary; there are gifts of speaking in strange tongues, but they will cease; there is knowledge, but it will pass. For our gifts of knowledge and of inspired messages are only partial; but when what is perfect comes, then what is partial will disappear. When I was a child, my speech, feelings, and thinking were all those of a child; now that I am an adult, I have no more use for childish ways. What we see now is like a dim image in a mirror; then we shall see face-to-face. What I know now is only partial; then it will be complete—as complete as God's knowledge of me. Meanwhile these three remain: faith, hope, and love; and the greatest of these is love. (1 Corinthians 13:4– 13 GNT)

But I tell you: Love your enemies and pray for those who persecute you. (Matthew 5:44 NIV)

As the Father has loved me, so have I loved you. Now remain in my love. (John 15:9–10 NIV)

I have been crucified with Christ and I no longer live, but Christ lives in me. The life I live in the body, I live by faith in the Son of God, who loved me and gave himself for me. (Galatians 2:20 NIV)

This is how we know what love is: Jesus Christ laid down his life for us. And we ought to lay down our lives for our brothers. (1 John 3:16 NIV)

But I tell you who hear me: Love your enemies, do good to those who hate you, bless those who curse you, pray for those who mistreat you. If someone strikes you on one cheek, turn to him the other also. If someone takes your cloak, do not stop him from taking your tunic. (Luke 6:27–30 NIV)

On the contrary: "If your enemy is hungry, feed him; if he is thirsty, give him something to drink. In doing this, you will heap burning coals on his head." Do not be overcome by evil, but overcome evil with good. (Romans 12:20– 21 NIV)

"In your anger do not sin": Do not let the sun go down while you are still angry, and do not give the devil a foothold. (Ephesians 4:26, 27 NIV)

And over all these virtues put on love, which binds them all together in perfect unity. (Colossians 3:14 NIV)

Several times Jesus and the scriptures have advised us to love our enemies and to overcome evil with good so the devil will not have any part in us. "Now remain in my love" (John 15:9). This is the Lord's command. To be able to love this way, in spite of the hurt or offence, you need the help of the Holy Spirit because this is not an ordinary love. Humanly speaking, the natural person (that is, the person without Jesus in his life) will find it difficult to do this or understand this kind of love. This love is sacrificial. It gives itself up for the joy of others. It makes peace where there is none. God loved us so much that he gave us his all, in spite of who and what we were.

You cannot say you love God, whom you have not seen before, while you hate your brother, whom you see everyday.

> If anyone says, "I love God," yet hates his brother, he is a liar. For anyone who does not love his brother, whom he has seen, cannot love God, whom he has not seen. (1 John 4:20– 21 NIV)

When you are able to show love in the face of hurts and offences, there is no way bitterness will take root in your life, even if you struggle with it for a short time. Love covers a multitude of sins; therefore, pray that the Holy Spirit will give you what it takes to love that abusive husband or father of yours, that bully of a boss, that colleague who always looks down on you, or that step-mother who is a thorn in your flesh. Who knows what God can do with your love?

3.   **Let God always be the judge of your case every time you are hurt or offended.**

> He never sinned, never told a lie, never answered back when insulted; when he suffered he did not threaten to get even; he left his case in the hands of God who always judges fairly. (1 Peter 2:22–23 TLB)

Don't take revenge even though that may seem the only alternative to appease your anger. Vengeance is the Lord's. Know that God is the ultimate judge, however, you can also go to court for redress.

> I thought in my heart, "God will bring to judgment both the righteous and the wicked, for there will be a time for every activity, a time for every deed." (Ecclesiastes 3:17 NIV)

> For we must all appear before the judgment seat of Christ, that each one may receive what is due him for the things done while in the body, whether good or bad. (2 Corinthians 5:10 NIV)

4. **Thank God for all the good things you enjoy and stop concentrating on only the negative things happening to you.**

Be positive in your outlook and hold on to Romans 8:28: "And we know that in all things God works for the good of those who love him, who have been called according to his purpose." (NIV).

Think positively based on who you are in Christ. Avoid or try to kill the desire for revenge. In all things we must give thanks. You may want the offender to taste or go through whatever he or she made you go through. It will surprise you to know that life is not always fair. Sometimes those who offended you may seem to be doing fairly well in life. All the evil you pronounced or expected to happen to them after your thirty days fasting may never materialize. Just thank God that you are alive in spite of all that has happened.

5.   **Make every effort to confess your sins daily.**

> If we confess our sins, he is faithful and just and will forgive us our sins and purify us from all unrighteousness. (1 John 1:9 NIV)

> He who conceals his sins does not prosper, but whoever confesses and renounces them finds mercy. (Proverbs 28:13 NIV)

> I will set out and go back to my father and say to him: Father, I have sinned against heaven and against you. (Luke 15:18 NIV)

The confession and repentance of the prodigal son was evidenced in his going back home.

> He himself bore our sins in his body on the tree, so that we might die to sins and live for righteousness; by his wounds you have been healed. (1 Peter 2:24 NIV)

> Blessed are those who hunger and thirst for righteousness, for they shall be filled. (Matthew 5:8 NIV)

Daily sincere confessions of sins (not the routine or scheduled confessions) will leave no room for lingering anger to fester into bitternes with time. If you are forgiven on daily basis, you are likely to appreciate what it means to forgive. When you hunger and desire righteousness daily, bitterness—sin—will have no place in your life. Repentance must follow confession. Matthew 3:8 tells us that we must "produce fruit in keeping with repentance" (NIV). If repentance is not seen in a new life or new fruit as evidence, then there is no point.

6.   **Guard your thoughts and allow yourself to be healed**

> For it is God's will that by doing good you should silence the ignorant talk of foolish men. (1 Peter 2:15 NIV)

> Above all else, guard your heart, for it is the wellspring of life. (Proverbs 4:23 NIV)

> Finally, brothers, whatever is true, whatever is noble, whatever is right, whatever is pure, whatever is lovely, whatever is admirable—if anything is excellent or praiseworthy—think about such things. (Philippians 4:8 NIV)

> The sinful mind is hostile to God. It does not submit to God's law, nor can it do so. Those controlled by the sinful nature cannot please God. (Romans 8:7–8 NIV)

> Blessed are the pure in heart, for they will see God. (Matthew 5:8 NIV)

When you refuse to allow evil thoughts to linger in your mind and spirit, bitterness will surely not take root in you. Let your thoughts be about excellent or praiseworthy things, and allow the Holy Spirit to heal your hurts instead of holding on to those impure thoughts of revenge and wickedness. Learn to be pure in heart, please God, and strive to be like Jesus on a daily basis.

7.   **Fear God.**

Show proper respect to everyone: Love the brotherhood of believers, fear God, honor the king. (1 Peter 2:17 NIV)

He said in a loud voice, "Fear God and give him glory, because the hour of his judgment has come." (Revelation 14:7 NIV)

Whatever happens, conduct yourselves in a manner worthy of the gospel of Christ. (Philippians 1:27 NIV)

The fear of God, the Bible says, is the beginning of wisdom. The fear of God will keep you from harbouring the evil of bitterness in your heart. As stated in Philippians 1:27, no matter what happens, conduct yourself in such a way that Christ will be honoured.

8.   **Put on the full armour of God daily.**

Put on all the armor that God gives you, so that you will be able to stand up against the Devil's evil tricks. For we are not fighting against human beings but against the wicked spiritual forces in the heavenly world, the rulers, authorities, and cosmic powers of this dark age. So put on God's armor now! Then when the evil day comes, you will be able to resist the enemy's attacks; and after fighting to the end, you will still hold your ground.

So stand ready, with truth as a belt tight around your waist, with righteousness as your breastplate, and as your shoes the readiness to announce the Good News of peace. At all times carry faith as a shield; for with it you will be able to put out all the burning arrows shot by the Evil One. And accept salvation as a helmet, and the word of God as the sword which the Spirit gives you. Do all this in prayer, asking for God's help. Pray on every occasion, as the Spirit leads. For this reason keep alert and never give up; pray always for all God's people. (Ephesians 6:11–18 GNT)

When you are fully prepared all the time against the attacks of the devil, you can always take a stand against his schemes. Bitterness is a scheme of the devil; therefore, by taking up the helmet of salvation and the sword of the spirit, which is the word of God, you will be able to deal with it before it manifests. The devil will always challenge your dependence on the word of God making it seem ineffective; however, you will have to stand your ground and hold on to the word. You cannot fight bitterness without the word of God if you call yourself a Christian.

9.   **Pray for help.**

Do not be anxious about anything, but in everything, by prayer and petition, with thanksgiving, present your requests to God. And the peace of God, which transcends all understanding, will guard your hearts and your minds in Christ Jesus. (Philippians 4:6–7 NIV)

Pray without ceasing. Prayer will always keep you in touch with heaven, where your ability to fight anger and bitterness comes from. In prayer you maintain a holy relationship with God, and this relationship has no room for anger and bitterness.

Praying about any potential situation that could result in bitterness will help nip the possibility in the bud. Deal with that annoying boss, cheating spouse, school bully, the in-laws who will not let you have any peace, job loss, and all other problems in prayer. When you win in the spirit, the physical will follow suit no matter how long it takes.

Prayer can give you insight as to what you are dealing with before it overtakes you. When you know what you are dealing with and its agenda, it becomes possible, or easier, for you to do something to avoid the intended or expected consequences.

Persistent prayer will keep at bay the owner of bitterness out of your life. When he has no way to download his negativity in you, there is no way he can infect you with a virus. Jesus said, "The prince of this world is coming. He has no hold over me" (John 14:30 NIV). The prince of the world is the devil. You can avoid being bitter when you don't allow the devil to have any part in you. This is the reason why you seriously need the Holy Spirit to help you on a daily basis, so you can keep the devil at bay.

10. **Your dream must make you forget about offense.**

When your dream is connected to somebody, an offense from that person should not cut your dream short, no matter what. Read the story about Elijah ascending to Heaven:

And it came to pass, when the Lord was about to take up Elijah into heaven by a whirlwind, that Elijah went with Elisha from Gilgal. Then Elijah said to Elisha, "Stay here, please, for the Lord has sent me on to Bethel."

But Elisha said, "As the Lord lives, and as your soul lives, I will not leave you!" So they went down to Bethel.

Now the sons of the prophets who were at Bethel came out to Elisha, and said to him, "Do you know that the Lord will take away your master from over you today?"

And he said, "Yes, I know; keep silent!"

Then Elijah said to him, "Elisha, stay here, please, for the Lord has sent me on to Jericho."

But he said, "As the Lord lives, and as your soul lives, I will not leave you!" So they came to Jericho.

Now the sons of the prophets who were at Jericho came to Elisha and said to him, "Do you know that the Lord will take away your master from over you today?"

So he answered, "Yes, I know; keep silent!"

Then Elijah said to him, "Stay here, please, for the Lord has sent me on to the Jordan."

But he said, "As the Lord lives, and as your soul lives, I will not leave you!" So the two of them went on. (2 Kings 2:1–6 NKJV)

Elisha could have taken offense at the way Elijah was treating him. He could have been angry at the company of prophets who thought he was daft not to know what was going on around him. However, because he knew what he was looking for, he never allowed bitterness to come in to cut short his desire for a double portion of the anointing on Elijah.

11. Believe you can do it.

Believe you can avoid being bitter. You can do all things through Christ who strengthens you, and with God all things are possible according to his will.

12. Learn to laugh at yourself sometimes.

Don't always take life too seriously and make it too rigid. Be a little flexible and make room for the unexpected. Laughter is said to be good for our health. It relaxes the whole body and boosts the immune system by increasing the immune cells and decreasing stress hormones. It has also been found that laughter increases the functionality of blood vessels, thereby increasing the blood flow to the heart. This in turn prevents heart problems. Do yourself this favour.

13. Renew your mind on daily basis.

In order to change your focus from the one who offended you, it is imperative for you to refocus your attention on Christ with the word of God.

14. Deal with the bad emotional habit of unforgiveness on a daily basis.

If you do this on a daily basis, you will not need to deal with any issue of bitterness at a later date. A bad habit can be changed only when it is replaced with a good one. You cannot just cut out bad habits without replacing them. A vacuum will be created and more bad habits will come in.

If we are what we repeatedly do, then you will be a bitter person with repeated unforgiveness in your life if you allow your current actions to become your habits. This will then become your destiny.

Chapter 15

HOW TO DEAL WITH BITTERNESS

In the previous chapter I said that it is better to prevent than to cure, but if for any reason you were not able to prevent yourself from getting into the state of bitterness, the only alternative is to cure it, which may be more difficult. However, it is possible.

Anything causing bitterness in your life is an agent of change. Are you in control of the change process? Change is part of the growth process, positive or negative. Without change we will always be the same. That is why you have to decide at this point in time that enough is enough—you want to change your emotional and psychological imprisonment for a better life. Until you decide that enough is enough, the situation will control you. You must take control. Before change can take place there must be an awareness that there is the need for change. If there is no awareness that something needs to be changed, there will be no desire for it. It therefore follows that desire must follow awareness. Being aware without a desire for change is useless. You may also have the desire, but if you don't have the knowledge for effecting the change, nothing will be achieved. That is why I have set out to give you some of the knowledge you will need to help you uproot bitterness from your life:

1. **To deal with bitterness, you must first of all accept that there is something wrong. You are in the Prison of Bitterness.**

   You must admit that you are bitter and need to get rid of it. Can you get rid of something you don't accept is wrong with you, or is even in your life? Hiding your bitterness and making everything seem to be all right will not help. Refusing to accept the fact that you have the bitterness disease closes the door for any meaningful resolution. Accepting the fact is half the battle won. This may be a bitter pill to swallow, but you have no choice if you really want to deal with bitterness. Take responsibility for whatever role you played. This is not to blame yourself but to correct whatever mistake you might have made.

2. **Confess unequivocally how you feel about the person who hurt you to the Lord.**

   Be true to God and yourself. Let your pain and frustration out to him. He understands. Ask the Holy Spirit to search your heart and reveal all the hidden hurts and resentments, and you will be surprised at what will follow if you are really sincere. "Tremble and do not sin; when you are on your beds, search your hearts and be silent" (Psalm 4:4 NIV). "Search me, God, and know my heart; test me and know my anxious thoughts" (Psalm 139:23 NIV).

3. **Acknowledge that you have sinned, and ask God for forgiveness.**

Shimei, after disgracing himself with the explosion of his bitterness, came to his senses one day and went to David to ask for forgiveness. This is what makes the difference between Absalom and Shimei. Absalom never regretted what he did or asked for forgiveness. You will save yourself from the wrath of God for your sin of bitterness if you repent and ask for forgiveness. It will not cost you anything except maybe your pride. Your repentance must be seen in a new transformed life and behaviour—the fruit of repentance (Matthew 3:8 NIV).

> Shimei son of Gera, the Benjamite from Bahurim, hurried down with the men of Judah to meet King David. With him were a thousand Benjamites, along with Ziba, the steward of Saul's household, and his fifteen sons and twenty servants. They rushed to the Jordan, where the king was. They crossed at the ford to take the king's household over and to do whatever he wished.

> When Shimei son of Gera crossed the Jordan, he fell prostrate before the king and said to him, "May my lord not hold me guilty. Do not remember how your servant did wrong on the day my lord the king left Jerusalem. May the king put it out of his mind. For I your servant know that I have sinned, but today I have come here as the first of the whole house of Joseph

to come down and meet my lord the king." (2 Samuel 19:16–20 NIV)

Why should you remain and die in your sin and go to hell? Repent and live!

Therefore, O house of Israel, I will judge you, each one according to his ways, declares the Sovereign Lord. Repent! Turn away from all your offenses; then sin will not be your downfall. Rid yourselves of all the offenses you have committed, and get a new heart and a new spirit. Why will you die, O house of Israel? For I take no pleasure in the death of anyone, declares the Sovereign Lord. Repent and live! (Ezekiel 18:30–32 NIV)

4. **After asking for forgiveness from God, you have to forgive yourself and those who hurt or offended you.**

Learn to forgive others and yourself. Unforgiveness hurts you more than the offender. Find out what role you played in bringing about this situation, and find ways to stop it from happening again. After you forgive, you must not bring the issue up again. Constant reference to the offence will always ignite passions.

If my people, who are called by my name, will humble themselves and pray and seek my face and turn from their wicked ways, then will I hear from heaven and will forgive their sin and will heal their land. (2 Chronicles 7:14–15 NIV)

For if you forgive men when they sin against you, your heavenly Father will also forgive you.

But if you do not forgive men their sins, your Father will not forgive your sins. (Matthew 6:14–15 NIV)

Bear with each other and forgive whatever grievances you may have against one another. Forgive as the Lord forgave you. (Colossians 3:13–14 NIV)

5. **Pray for the one who hurt you.**

It may not be easy, but praying for the one who hurt you will help take away the venom in you and gradually replace it with the love of God.

But I tell you: Love your enemies and pray for those who persecute you, that you may be sons of your Father in heaven. He causes his sun to rise on the evil and the good, and sends rain on the righteous and the unrighteous. (Matthew 5:44–46 NIV)

6. **Stop the pity party and ask for help.**

It will be all right to allow family members to give you support where possible. Accept nice things that are said about you, and don't be too harsh with yourself. Talk to a godly counsellor for help. After that stop telling your story to everyone. It will not help you. It will only rekindle your hurt and perpetuate the bitter feeling.

7. **Don't give up on yourself.**

So far as human beings continue to be what they are, people whom you consider as friends or close associates will continue to hurt or offend you. Try to spend time with others and move on with your life. You cannot continue to live as an island. Tell yourself you are able. Maybe changing your perspective on the situation as it is today, and looking at it in a different way especially with the future in mind will be helpful.

8.   You need a new understanding and a new attitude.

Change your mind. If you don't get rid of your bitterness, it may last through generations. You are responsible for all you do, say, think, and feel, and you have the power to respond to situations in whatever way you choose. The power to get rid of bitterness in your life lies within you. The choice is yours. Bitterness is not an imposition; it is a choice. Choose to get rid of it even if it hurts or takes some time. What about critically considering the opportunities you have today, and the impact of your bitter state? To help yourself, you can take on other new interests that will demand a new attitude. This will help shift your focus for a while.

Anyway, it is also a command to rid yourself of bitterness: "Get rid of all bitterness, rage and anger, brawling and slander, along with every form of malice" (Ephesians 4:31 NIV).

"I can do everything through him who gives me strength" (Philippians 4:13 NIV). May God give you the strength to go for change and prevail through the process.

9.   Every misfortune is said to be a blessing in disguise.

See your situation as an opportunity to bring something positive into your life.

> Now I want you to know, brothers, that what has happened to me has really served to advance the gospel. As a result, it has become clear throughout the whole palace guard and to everyone else that I am in chains for Christ. Because of my chains, most of the brothers in the Lord have been encouraged to speak the word of God more courageously and fearlessly. (Philippians 1:12–14 NIV)

Paul had been imprisoned because of the gospel. During his imprisonment, an entire palace guard got to know about Christ, and they changed. Additionally, most of the Christians around were encouraged and emboldened to speak fearlessly for Christ. Your testimony of change can change someone else' life.

"Be very careful, then, how you live—not as unwise but as wise, making the most of every opportunity, because the days are evil" (Ephesians 5:15–17 NIV). It is God's plan and purpose that his people should showcase his goodness and power in their lives. A believer's everyday life and everything about him or her should be a banner that proclaims what God has done in his or her life. When this happens, it is likely that others may want to believe in God, but often we are a stumbling block. Many a time our lives, actions, and speech do not proclaim Christ or showcase his goodness. We would be better off if we genuinely and consciously surrendered our lives to Jesus. His word purifies our lives on daily basis and helps us to become a testimony that proclaims what God has done.

Part 4

CONCLUSIONS

You are better off without bitterness.

Chapter 16

BLESSINGS OF FORGIVENESS

Think about this. What would have happened if Absalom had forgiven his brother Amnon after the two years of wondering in the wilderness of bitterness? When you forgive, you receive the following blessings and more from God as a covenant child.

1. **You receive God's forgiveness.**

   But if you do no forgive men their sins, your Father will not forgive your sins. (Matthew 6:15 NIV)

2. **You also receive answers to your prayers.**

   Therefore I tell you, whatever you ask for in prayer, believe that you have received it, and it will be yours. And when you stand praying, if you hold anything against anyone, forgive him, so that your Father in heaven may forgive you your sins. (Mark 11:24–25VNIV)

3. **You remain in the love of Christ.**

    If you obey my commands, you will remain in my love, just as I have obeyed my Father's commands and remain in his love. (John 15:10)

4. **You pass from spiritual death to life.**

    We know that we have passed from death to life, because we love our brothers. Anyone who does not love remains in death. (1 John 3:14 NIV)

5. **You prove that you love Jesus.**

    Whoever has my commands and obeys them, he is the one who loves me. He who loves me will be loved by my Father, and I too will love him and show myself to him. (John 14:21 NIV)

6. **You remain in Christ and bear fruit.**

    You are already clean because of the word I have spoken to you. Remain in me, and I will remain in you. No branch can bear fruit by itself; it must remain in the vine. Neither can you bear fruit unless you remain in me. (John 15:3–4 NIV)

7. **Fellowship with God is restored.**

    > But if you do not forgive men their sins, your
    > Father will not forgive your sins. (Matthew
    > 6:15 NIV)

    When the father does not forgive you then fellowship with
    him is broken. Forgiving others restores fellowship with
    the father.

8. **When you forgive and are forgiven, it frustrates the
    work of the devil.**

    > "In your anger do not sin": Do not let the sun go
    > down while you are still angry, and do not give
    > the devil a foothold. (Ephesians 4:26–27 NIV)

    > If you forgive anyone, I also forgive him. And
    > what I have forgiven—if there was anything
    > to forgive—I have forgiven in the sight of
    > Christ for your sake, in order that Satan might
    > not outwit us. For we are not unaware of his
    > schemes. (2 Corinthians 2:10–11 NIV)

    When you forgive and you are forgiven, the devil loses his
    grip on your life. The doorway into your life is shut in his
    face. His access card is taken from him. He cannot down-
    load into your life again.

9. **You will have peace with God and the person you have
    forgiven.**

    You may even be in a position to bring that person to
    Christ by your act of forgiveness if that person does not
    know him.

> Now bands of raiders from Aram had gone out and had taken captive a young girl from Israel, and she served Naaman's wife. She said to her mistress, "If only my master would see the prophet who is in Samaria! He would cure him of his leprosy." (2 Kings 5:2–3 NIV)

This young slave girl violently abducted by the Syrians from her parents in Israel did not harbour any bitterness against her captors. She went to the extent of not only forgiving them but also initiated the healing process of her slave master. At the end of the healing process, the master became a believer in the God of Israel.

10. **You will be one experience richer.**

By this experience you will have what it takes to deal with anger next time it pops up and even help other people to do same.

11. **Better health.**

You will cut out so many diseases that are aggravated by stress caused by unforgiveness.

12. **You cease to be a victim; rather, you become a victor over evil escaping from the prison of bitterness.**

The story of Joseph clearly shows us that, when you forgive, you win over evil. Joseph forgave his brothers who meant evil by their actions and by that saved a whole nation of Israel from extinction through famine.

Joseph Revealed to His Brothers

Then Joseph could not restrain himself before all those who stood by him, and he cried out, "Make everyone go out from me!" So no one stood with him while Joseph made himself known to his brothers. And he wept aloud, and the Egyptians and the house of Pharaoh heard it.

Then Joseph said to his brothers, "I am Joseph; does my father still live?" But his brothers could not answer him, for they were dismayed in his presence. And Joseph said to his brothers, "Please come near to me." So they came near. Then he said: "I am Joseph your brother, whom you sold into Egypt. But now, do not therefore be grieved or angry with yourselves because you sold me here; for God sent me before you to preserve life. For these two years the famine has been in the land, and there are still five years in which there will be neither plowing nor harvesting. And God sent me before you to preserve a posterity for you in the earth, and to save your lives by a great deliverance. (Genesis 45:1–7 NIV)

13. Your righteousness will help your deliverance from all troubles.

The righteous cry out, and the Lord hears them;
he delivers them from all their troubles. (Psalm 34:17 NIV)

Bitterness is sin, but it is sad that many people do not see it as such. This is a terrible deception. Most people can't see this until they are Destroyed (imprisoned) by the sin they pursue. As a believer or a non-believer, you can have the advantage of believing God's word. You don't have to learn by the hard experience of the destructive results of sin.

Chapter 17

CONCLUSION

I totally agree with Gandhi that forgiveness is for strong people. It was Gandhi who said, "The weak can never forgive. Forgiveness is the attribute of the strong."[35] When you look at the life of a person like Nelson Mandela, a former president of South Africa, you see that, if he had not been a strong man, he would have found it difficult to forgive the perpetrators of apartheid in South Africa. He had every reason—and great support—for vengeance on the whites who incarcerated him for the greater part of his productive life and made life unbearable for the black majority in his country. He, however, resisted vengeance and extended an olive branch to his opponents.

The virtues of kindness and forgiveness are to be put in place of the sins of anger and malice and their close relative, bitterness. Pastor Paul Tautges writes in his book, *Counsel One Another: A Theology of Personal Discipleship,* that a bitter person is usually someone who refuses to forgive others or one who will not humbly submit to God's sovereignty through the painful trials of life.[36]

Jesus, our master and greatest example, even at the time his killers were driving the cruel metal into his palms, was still strong enough in character and attitude to forgive them. Friend, we should see to it that we do not have an unbelieving and a sinful heart that will take us away from the Lord.

> Beware, brethren, lest there be in any of you an evil heart of unbelief in departing from the living God; but exhort one another daily, while it is called "Today," lest any of you be hardened through the deceitfulness of sin. For we have become partakers of Christ if we hold the beginning of our confidence steadfast to the end, while it is said: "Today, if you will hear His voice, Do not harden your hearts as in the rebellion."

Failure of the Wilderness Wanderers

> For who, having heard, rebelled? Indeed, was it not all who came out of Egypt, led by Moses? Now with whom was He angry forty years? Was it not with those who sinned, whose corpses fell in the wilderness? And to whom did He swear that they would not enter His rest, but to those who did not obey? So we see that they could not enter in because of unbelief. (Hebrews 3:12–19 NKJV)

> Therefore, since the promise of entering his rest still stands, let us be careful that none

of you be found to have fallen short of it. (Hebrews 4:1 NIV)

It still remains that some will enter that rest, and those who formerly had the gospel preached to them did not go in, because of their disobedience. Therefore God again set a certain day, calling it Today, when a long time later he spoke through David, as was said before: "Today, if you hear his voice, do not harden your hearts." (Hebrews 4:6–7 NIV)

I believe that, as you read this book, you heard the voice of God speaking and pleading with you to forgive and let go. Today, if you have heard his voice, what are you waiting for? Do not harden your heart because you may not have this opportunity to obey the voice of God in this matter again. This is your chance to bring your pain to an end. If you have to cry, let it out, and after that obey God and see yourself free from this destroyer. Shame the devil by destroying his property in your life.

Finally, brothers, wha ever is true, whatever is noble, whatever is right, whatever is pure, whatever is lovely, whatever is admirable—if anything is excellent or praiseworthy—think about such things. (Philippians 4:8 NIV)

Now all has been heard; Here is the conclusion of the matter: Fear God and keep his commandments, for this is the whole duty of man. For God will bring every deed into judgment, including every hidden thing, whether it is good or evil. (Ecclesiastes 12:13– 14 NIV)

Are you ready for this judgement?

Free yourself from this prison of bitterness. Destroy the destroyer with your forgiveness and gain your peace and freedom. God bless you for your obedience.

Chapter 18

A CRY FOR HELP!

You may pray this prayer if you need help. After the second sentence, you can add specific information about what is causing your bitter feelings:

> Father, I have sinned against you and I confess that I am a sinner. I have allowed bitterness to destroy my life, my relationship with you and …

> Please have mercy, forgive me, and wash me with the blood of Jesus Christ shed on the cross at Calvary. Come into my life, Lord Jesus, and be my Lord and Saviour. Please write my name in the Lamb's Book of Life. Make me your child, and rule over my life.

> I thank you for forgiving and saving me. Amen!

References

INTRODUCTION

1   Thinkexist.com, Maya Angelou quotes, *http://thinkexist.com/quotes/maya angelou/*, accessed 2 May 2011.

CHAPTER 1

2   Thinkexist.com, Martin Luther King, Jr. quotes," http://thinkexist.com/quotes/martin_luther_king,_jr., accessed 2 May 2011.

CHAPTER 2

3   Right Words, Quotes by Cesare Pavese, http://www.right-words.eu/quotes/quote-details/21482/if-you-wish- to-travel-far-and-fast-travel-light-21482, accessed 6 October 2016.

4   I-Love-Quotes.com, George Bernard Shaw Quote, *http://www.1-love-quotes.com/quote/817401*, accessed 8 September 2011.

CHAPTER 3

5   Cerminaro, Anthony, A Soul Searching" (23 May 2007) http://acerminaro.blogspot.com/2006/01/quotes-from-henri-jm-nouwen.html, accessed 6 October 2016

6   Lee, David Michael, Hints of a Legacy Left Behind, "Holding on to Your Faith … Even When it Doesn't Make Sense" 20 February 2010, accessed 30 July 2013

CHAPTER 4

7   Brainy Quote, James A. Baldwin Quotes, http://www. brainyquote.com/quotes/authors/j/james_a_baldwin. html, 10 September 2013

8   Your Dictionary, Hesoid Quotes, *http://quotes.your dictionary.com/author/hesiod/62328, 10 September 2013*

CHAPTER 5

9   Search Quotes, Shirley Hufsteddler Quotes and Sayings, http://www.searchquotes.com/quotation/You_don%27t_make_progress_by_standing_on_the_sidelines,_whimpering_and_complaining._You_make_progress_/228165/, 4 October 2013

CHAPTER 6

10   Thinkexist.com, Mahatma Gandhi Quotes, http://thinkexist. com/quotation/the_moment_the_slave_resolves_that_he_will_no/148519.html, 4 October 2013

CHAPTER 7

11   Tentmaker, Pride Quotes, http://www.tentmaker.org/Quotes/pride_quotes.html, 6 January 2014

12   Brainy Quote, Fulton J. Sheen Quotes, *http://www. brainy-quote.com/quotes/quotes/f/fultonjsh155511.html,* 15 January 2014

13   Good Reads, Joan Didion Quotable Quote: *http://www. goodreads.com/quotes/484702-most-of-our-platitudes- not-withstanding-self-deception-rem ins-the-most- difficult, 15 January 2014*

CHAPTER 8

14   Brainy Quote, Wellington Mara Quotes, http://www. brainyquote.com/quotes/quotes/w/wellington223885. html, 15 January 2014

CHAPTER 9

15   Thinkexist.com, Mother Teresa of Cucuta Quotes, http:// thinkexist.com/quotation/we_think_sometimes_that_ poverty_is_only_being/216176.html, 15 January 2014

16   AZ Quotes, W. Somerset Maugham, *http://www.azquotes. com/quote/558702, 26 January 2014*

CHAPTER 10

17   Wisdom Quotes, Elizabeth Drew Quote, http://www. wis-domquotes.com/quote/elizabeth-drew-1.html, 27 January 2014

18   Brainy Quote, Lou Holtz Quotes, *http://www.brainyquote. com/quotes/quotes/l/louholtz450788.html,* 27 January 2014

19   Personal-development.com, *http://www.personal-dedevel-opment.com/chuck/frustration.htm,* 18 December 2016

CHAPTER 11

20   IZ Quotes, Dorothy Parker Quote, http://izquotes.com/
quote/331825, 15 December 2016

21   Thinkexist.com, John Powell Quotes, *http://thinkexist.
com/quotation/human beings-like plants-grow in the soil
of/194439.html*, 20 June 2014

22   Brainy Quote, Rejection Quotes, *http: /www.brainyquote.
com/quotes/keywords/rejection.html#ixzz1M83Y3xPu*, 20
June 2014

23   Thinkexist.com Rejection Quotes, *http://thinkexist.com/
quotations/rejection/*, 21 June 2014

CHAPTER 12

24   The Quote Garden, Quotations about Jealousy & envy,
http://www.quotegarden.com/jealousy.html, 19 July 201

CHAPTER 13

25   Brainy Quote, Robert Menzies Quotes, http://www. brainy-
quote.com/quotes/quotes/r/robertmenz117536. html, 21
April 2011

26   Thinkexist.com, Harry Emerson Fosdick Quotes, *http://
thinkexist.com/quotation/bitterness imprisons life- love
releases it/208684.html, 25 April 2011*

27   Thinkexist.com, Pessimism Quotes, *http://thinkexist.com/
quotations/pessimism/*, accessed 25 April 2011.

28   Thinkexist.com, Prevention Quotes, *http://thinkexist.com/
quotes/with/keyword/prevention /*, 25 April 2011.

29   Famous Quotes & Authors, Self-Pity Quotes and
Quotations,   *http://www.famousquotesandauthors.com/
topics/self pity quotes.html,* 25 April 2011.

30 Thinkexist.com, Prevention Quotes, *http://thinkexist.com/ quotes/with/keyword/prevention/,* 25 April 2011.

31 Quote Album, Self-Pity Quotes *http: /www.quotealbum. com/quote/z9cNQ/self-pity-is-one-of-the-most-dangerous-forms-of-se,* accessed 9 September 2011.

32 Thinkexist.com, Mother Teresa of Calcutta Quotes, *http:// thinkexist.com/quotation/if you judge peopleyou have no time to love them/216200.htm,* accessed 8 October 2011.

CHAPTER 14

33 Thinkexist.com, Henry de Bracton Quotes, http:// thinkexist.com/quotation/an_ounce_of_prevention_is_worth_a_pound_of_cure/208042.html, accessed 8 October 2011.

34 Thinkexist.com, Paul Boese Quotes, *http://thinkexist. com/ quotation/forgiveness does not change the past-but it does/9267.html,* 8 October 2011.

CHAPTER 17

35 The Quotations Page, http://www.quotationspage.com/ quote/2188.html, accessed 9 August 2011.

36 Tautges, Paul, *Counsel One Another: A Theology of Personal Discipleship* (Leominster, UK, 2009).